The People of
BELFAST
1600-1799

David Dobson

CLEARFIELD

Copyright © 2016
by David Dobson
All Rights Reserved.

Printed for Clearfield Company by
Genealogical Publishing Company
Baltimore, Maryland
2016

ISBN 978-0-8063-5788-1

INTRODUCTION

Belfast lies at the head of Belfast Lough. In the medieval time it was a settlement lying within the jurisdiction of the Earl of Ulster known as *Beal Feirste* which is Irish Gaelic signifying 'the mouth of the sandy ford'.

The transformation of Belfast from being a small village to a significant city began with it being granted a Royal Charter in 1613 thereby making it semi-autonomous and allowed economic expansion to occur. At that date the population is reckoned to have been around one thousand, two centuries later it probably had about twenty two thousand inhabitants. For a period Belfast was under the influence of the Chichester family. Sir Arthur Chichester appointed the early Sovereigns [mayors] and selected the burgesses who formed the town council..

It was largely during the period of the Plantation of Ulster, ordered by King James I [VI of Scotland] in the early seventeenth century, that the indigenous Catholic Irish population saw the arrival of Presbyterian Scots and Anglican English and Manxmen. Huguenots fleeing from oppression in France were later arrivals. Emigration from Ulster to America, through the port of Belfast, grew in size during the eighteenth century, emigrants consisting mainly of Protestants availing themselves of space on merchant ships belonging to Belfast merchants.

Two centuries after the granting of the Royal Charter the population had expanded to around twenty two thousand. Belfast developed trading links with Scotland, England, France and Spain at an early date, and in the late seventeenth century with the West Indies and the American Colonies. It exported local agricultural produce, such as beef, butter and hides. Its imports included coal, fruit, wine, sugar and tobacco. Flax seed from Philadelphia and New York was another import, and the resulting flax became the raw material for the production of valuable Irish linen cloth, the manufacture of which, though produced in Ireland for millennium, was greatly enhanced in quality by Huguenot skills.

This book identifies residents of Belfast living during the seventeenth and eighteenth centuries, and is based mainly on primary sources in Ireland, Scotland, England, and elsewhere. Researchers will find a list of those sources at the back of the volume.

David Dobson, Dundee, Scotland, 2015.

The Sally sails from Belfast to Philadelphia, May 1762

THE PEOPLE OF BELFAST, 1600-1799

ABERCROMBY, JAMES, a merchant on the Elizabeth of Belfast 1690. [NRS.E72.12.16]

ADAIR, JAMES, in Belfast, a lease in Broad Street, Belfast, 1746. [PRONI.D298.12/13/14]; a banker in Belfast, 1752. [TBB][UJA.II.1.161]; a merchant in Belfast in 1758. [PRONI.D354.1010]

ADAIR, Lieutenant JOSEA, was admitted as a Freeman of Belfast in 1767. [TBB]

ADAIR, PATRICK, born 1624, a Presbyterian minister in Belfast, died 1695. [NLS.Wodrow Folio.xxvi.52]

ADAIR, WILLIAM, in Belfast, 1661, [ICH] in Belfast, 1669. [PRONI.T307A]

ADAIR, WILLIAM, master of the Prosperity of Belfast 1689. [NRS.E72.19.15]; bound for the Canary Islands, 1690. [NRS.E72.3.21]

ADAMS, GILBERT, born 1791, in Belfast, died 1818. [Clifton Street MI]

ADAMS, JAMES, a farmer, was admitted as a Freeman of Belfast in 1728. [TBB]

ADAM. JOHN, master of the Mayflower of Belfast 1684. [NRS.E72.19.9]; master of the Friendship of Belfast 1710. [EUL.Laing ms490.120.1]

ADAMS, JOHN, master of the Hanover of Belfast 1736; master of the William and James of Belfast trading with Charleston, South Carolina, in 1737. [TNA.CO5.509]

ADAM, WILLIAM, master of the Prosperity of Belfast trading with the Canary Islands in 1689. [NRS.E72.3.18]

THE PEOPLE OF BELFAST, 1600-1799

A'DIDDELL, WILLIAM, a yarn merchant, son of Adam A'Diddell at the Falls, was admitted as a Freeman of Belfast in 1730. [TBB]

AFFLECK, WILLIAM, lease of Carrick, Peter's Hill, Belfast, in 1780. [PRONI.D298.50]

AGNEW, ANDREW, a merchant in Belfast, deeds, 1695. 1701. [NRS.RD2.78.724; RD4.89.975]

AGNEW, ANDREW, in Belfast, a lease, 1737. [PRONI.D298.10]

AGNEW, DAVID, a merchant on board the James of Belfast, at Barbados,1668. [ActsPCCol.755/1041]

AGNEW, GEORGE, a mealman, was admitted as a Free Commoner of Belfast in 1650. [TBB]; in Belfast, 1669. [PRONI.T307A]

AGNEW, JOHN, in Belfast, 1669. [PRONI.T307A]

AGNEW, PATRICK, in Belfast, 1669. [PRONI.T307A]

AGNEW, PATRICK, a merchant, was admitted as a Freeman of Belfast in 1731. [TBB]

AGNEW, ROBERT, master of the Andrew of Belfast 1682, 1684, 1689. [NRS.E72.19.5/6/14; E72.3.13]

AGNEW, THOMAS, a pupil at Lord Donegal's school in Belfast, 1686. [NRS.GD154.935/1915]

AGNES, THOMAS, a slater, was admitted as a Freeman of Belfast in 1726. [TBB]

AGNEW, ……, in the barony of Belfast, 1659. [C]

AICKEN, FRANCIS, born 1754, died 1826. [Clifton Street MI]

THE PEOPLE OF BELFAST, 1600-1799

AINSLEY, GEORGE, a skinner, was admitted as a Freeman of Belfast in 1731. [TBB]

ALDERDICE, FRANCES, born 1755, died 1803, [Clifton Street MI]

ALDERDICE, JAMES, born 1774, died 1812. [Clifton Street MI]

ALDRIDGE, ROBERT, a staymaker, was admitted as a Freeman of Belfast in 1731. [TBB]

ALEXANDER, GEORGE, a yeoman and a rioter in Belfast, 1614. [OB38]

ALEXANDER, JAMES, a tailor Freeman of Belfast, 1673. [TBB.128]

ALEXANDER, JOHN, born 1748, of Peter's Hill, died 1832. [Clifton Street MI]

ALEXANDER, JOHN, born 1735, of Ardmoulin, Belfast, died 1821. [Clifton Street MI]

ALEXANDER, JOHN, in Belfast, a letter, 1758. [PRONI.D354.682]

ALEXANDER, JOHN, a merchant in Belfast, was admitted as a Freeman of Belfast in 1760. [TBB]

ALEXANDER, ROBERT, a peruke-maker, was admitted as a Freeman of Belfast in 1730. [TBB]

ALEXANDER, WILLIAM, MD, in Belfast, a witness to the will of Hugh Wallace probate 1716 Dublin

ALLEN, ANDREW, was admitted as a Freeman of Belfast in 1777. [TBB]

ALLEN, HUGH, in Belfast, a lease, 1770. [PRONI.D509.432]

THE PEOPLE OF BELFAST, 1600-1799

ALLEN, JOHN, in Malone, a Freeman of Belfast, in 1783. [TBB]

ALLEN, MARGARET, born 1773, died 1790, daughter of William Allen, sister of William, Sarah, and Mary-Ann. [Shankill MI, Belfast]

ALLAN, ROBERT, a merchant in Belfast, 1725, 1726. [NRS.AC7.32.116; AC9.967]

ALLEN, SAMUEL, a merchant, was admitted as a Freeman of Belfast in 1727. [TBB]

ALLEN, WILLIAM, of Milewater, a gardener, was admitted as a Freeman of Belfast in 1747. [TBB]

ALLISON, ROBERT, master of the <u>Two Brothers of Belfast</u> 1683. [NRS.E72.12.8]

ALWOOD, JOHN, an adventurer who was granted land in the north-east and also the south-east quarter of the barony of Belfast, 1643. [SPI.1642-1659: 354]

AMYS, WILLIAM, master of the <u>Unicorn of Belfast</u> trading with the Leeward Islands and Virginia in 1675. [ActsPCCol.161`3-1680, no.1047]

ANDERSON, GEORGE, a merchant in Belfast, 1689, [RPCS.XIII.583]; was admitted as a burgess and guilds-brother of Ayr, 1697. [ABR]

ANDERSON, GEORGE, a merchant in Belfast, was admitted as a burgess and guilds-brother of Ayr in 1753. [ABR]

ANDERSON, HENRY, was admitted as a Freeman of Belfast in 1640. [TBB]

ANDERSON, HUGH, an innkeeper, was admitted as a Freeman of Belfast in 1729. [TBB]

THE PEOPLE OF BELFAST, 1600-1799

ANDERSON, HUGH, in Exchange Alley, Belfast, 1733-1763. [PRONI.D354.295]

ANDERSON, JAMES, a burgess of Belfast, 1639. [TBB]

ANDERSON, JAMES, a merchant or attorney of Belfast and Dublin, probate 1706.

ANDERSON, JOHN, in Belfast in 1645. [TBB]

ANDERSON, ROBERT, a merchant, was admitted as a Freeman of Belfast in 1731. [TBB]

ANDERSON, SARAH, born 1758, died 1761, daughter of William Anderson a bricklayer in Belfast. [Shankill MI, Belfast]

ANDERSON, THOMAS, a servant, was admitted as a Freeman of Belfast in 1729. [TBB]

ANDERSON, WILLIAM, a merchant, was admitted as a Freeman of Belfast, 1658. [TBB]

ANDERSON, …… widow of William Partridge in Belfast in 1647. [TBB]

ANDREWS, HUGH, a merchant, was admitted as a Freeman of Belfast in 1728. [TBB]; in Belfast, a deed, 1742. [PRONI.3254.296]

ANDREWS, THOMAS, in Belfast, died 1809, husband of Anne Forde, died 1814. [Clifton Street MI]

ANDREWS, WILLIAM, born 1749, died 1821, husband of Jane …., born 1748, died 1818, parents of John Andrews, born 1777, died 1837. [Shankill MI, Belfast]

APPLEWHITE, JOHN, a gentleman in Belfast in 1659. [C]

THE PEOPLE OF BELFAST, 1600-1799

APSLEY, ROBERT, a surgeon in Belfast, was admitted as a Freeman of Belfast in 1766. [TBB]

ARBUCKLE, JAMES, a merchant in Belfast, 1689, [RPCS.XIII.583]; trading with Virginia in 1692, [TNA.HCA.Exams. 80.Rex versus Scott]; was admitted as a burgess and guilds-brother of Glasgow in 1715, [GBR]; co-owner of the Friendship of Belfast bound for Charleston, South Carolina, in 1718, charter party, [PRONI.D354.370]; agent for the Prince Frederick bound for New England from Dublin in 1719, [Dublin Courant: 10.2.1719]; a merchant in Belfast, 1722. [NRS.AC9.849]

ARBUCKLE, JAMES, junior, a merchant, was admitted as a Freeman of Belfast in 1728. [TBB]; a merchant in Belfast, a bill of exchange, 1738. [PRONI.D354.431]

ARBUCKLE, JOHN, in Belfast, 1669. [PRONI.T307A]

ARBUCKLE, WILLIAM, a merchant on board the Marigold of Belfast bound for Madeira in 1690. [NRS.E72.19.22]; son of James Arbuckle, a merchant in Belfast, was admitted as a burgess and guilds-brother of Glasgow in 1715. [GBR]

ARCHIBALD, JAMES, a merchant, was admitted as a Freeman of Belfast in 1752. [TBB]

ARCHIBALD, SARAH, born 1769, died 1818. [Shankill MI, Belfast]

ARMSTRONG, JAMES, a linen-draper, was admitted as a Freeman of Belfast in 1728. [TBB]

ARMSTRONG, JAMES, a butcher, was admitted as a Freeman of Belfast in 1767. [TBB]

ARMSTRONG, JOHN, a merchant, was admitted as a Freeman of Belfast in 1739. [TBB]

THE PEOPLE OF BELFAST, 1600-1799

ARMSTRONG, NATHAN, a carpenter in Belfast, was admitted as a Freeman of Belfast in 1760. [TBB]

ARMSTRONG, ROBERT, a merchant in Belfast, trading with Spain and Gibraltar, 1734. [PRONI.D354.493]

ARMSTRONG, THOMAS, in Belfast, a lease in Gregg's Land, Belfast, 1792. [PRONI.D491.54]

ARNOLD, JOHN, a Notary Public in Belfast, a declaration, 1733. [PRONI.D354.420A]; an attorney in the borough court of Belfast in 1754, [TBB]; a burgess of Belfast, a letter 1754. [PRONI.D354.1007]; a letter, 1758. [PRONI.D354.346]

ARNOLD, THOMAS, a gentleman from Dromore, was admitted as a Freeman of Belfast in 1730. [TBB]

ARTHUR, ALEXANDER, a farmer in Belfast, a lease, 1685. [PRONI.D271.2]

ARTHUR, ALEXANDER, a gentleman in Belfast, witness to the will of Thomas McIlwain, probate Dublin 1777.

ARTHUR, CHARLES, master of the Charles of Belfast trading with Montserrat in 1691. [NRS.E72.19.21]

ARTHUR, ROBERT, master and merchant of the Jane and Sarah of Belfast 1691. [NRS.E72.19.22]; master of the Charles of Belfast trading with Montserrat and the West Indies, 1691. [NRS.E72.15.21]

ARTHUR, WILLIAM, a merchant in Belfast, was admitted as a Freeman of Belfast in 1760. [TBB]

ASH, JOHN, an adventurer who was granted land in the north-east and also the south-east quarter of the barony of Belfast, 1643. [SPI.1642-1659: 354]; a gentleman, who was admitted as a burgess of Belfast in 1642. [TBB]

THE PEOPLE OF BELFAST, 1600-1799

ASHMORE, Mrs SARAM, born 1741, widow of Samuel Ashmore a merchant in Belfast, died 1821. [Clifton Street MI]

ASMORE, WILLIAM, a burgess of Belfast, 1639. [TBB]

ASPINALL, RICHARD, a merchant, and a Citizen of London, was admitted as a Free Stapler of Belfast in 1647. [TBB]

ATCHINSON, Mrs JEAN, born 1775, wife of John Atchinson an Excise officer, died 5 April 1811. [Shankill MI, Belfast]

ATHOLL, WILLIAM, a smith, was admitted as a Freeman of Belfast in 1758. [TBB]

ATKINSON, JOHN, a tanner from Drogheda, was admitted as a Freeman of Belfast in 1727. [TBB]

ATKINSON, WILLIAM, was appointed Clerk of Belfast in 1796. [TBB]

AUCHENLECK, WILLIAM, born 1744, a Notary Public, died 1815, husband of Sarah Ann ......born 1753, died 1795. [Shankill MI, Belfast]

AUSTEN, GEORGE, servant to John Leithes the Sovereign of Belfast, was admitted as a Freeman of Belfast in 1639. [TBB]

AYSHE, JOHN, a burgess of Belfast in 1632. [TBB]

BACHELOR, ROBERT, was admitted as a Freeman of Belfast in 1640. [TBB]

BAGLEY, THOMAS, a merchant, was admitted as a Freeman of Belfast in 1748. [TBB]

BAILLIE, JAMES, master of the <u>Mary of Belfast</u> bound for Barbados, 1726. [NRS.AC9.967]

THE PEOPLE OF BELFAST, 1600-1799

BAILLIE, WALTER, in Belfast in 1645. [TBB]

BAIRD, JAMES, born 1757, died 1809, husband of Ann Baird, born 1751, died 1809. [Clifton Street MI]

BAKER, JOHN, in Belfast, a lease in North Street, Belfast, 1751. [PRONI.D298.18]

BALAQUIER, JOHN, a burgess of Belfast, a letter 1754. [PRONI.D354.1007]

BALL, ENOCH, a nailer, was admitted as a Freeman of Belfast in 1727. [TBB]

BALLANTYNE, ARCHIBALD, in Belfast, 1669. [PRONI.T307A]

BANKS, ELIZABETH, in Belfast, a lease in Broad Street, Belfast, 1746. [PRONI.D298.12/13]

BANKS, ROBERT, in Belfast, reference to in Richard Hodgkinson's will of 1720, probate Dublin,

BANKS, ROBERT, son of Sovereign Stewart Banks, was admitted as a Freeman of Belfast in 1758. [TBB]

BANKS, STEWART, Sovereign of Belfast, 1756. [TBB]; a burgess of Belfast, a letter 1754. [PRONI.D354.1007]

BANKS, THOMAS, in Belfast, 1720, see Richard Hodgkinson's will; a lease of North Street, Belfast, 1726. [PRONI.D295.4]; a burgess of Belfast, a letter 1754. [PRONI.D354.1007]

BANKS, THOMAS, son of the Sovereign, was admitted as a Freeman of Belfast in 1758. [TBB]

BARCLAY, JOHN, a shopkeeper, was admitted as a Freeman of Belfast in 1731. [TBB]

THE PEOPLE OF BELFAST, 1600-1799

BARKER, JOHN, in Belfast, a lease in 1770. [PRONI.D509.434]

BARKER, THOMAS, was admitted as a Freeman of Belfast in 1643. [TBB]

BARNES, EDMUND, a blacksmith, was admitted as a Freeman of Belfast in 1639. [TBB]

BARNES, JOHN, servant to John Leithes the Sovereign of Belfast, was admitted as a Freeman of Belfast in 1639. [TBB]

BARNETT, JAMES, in Belfast, an account, 1732. [PRONI.D354.482]

BASHFORD, JAMES, a carpenter, was admitted as a Freeman of Belfast in 1752. [TBB]

BASHFORD, THOMAS MARSHALL, born 1776, a merchant from Belfast, applied for naturalisation in South Carolina in 1807. [NARA.M1183]

BATESON, THOMAS, born 1704, eldest son of Robert Bateson in Lancashire, a banker in Belfast, 1752. [TBB]; a merchant in Belfast in 1758. [PRONI.D354.1010]; he married Margaret White, widow of William Hartley in Dublin, in 1747, and died in 1791. [UJA.II.1.161]

BATSFORD, JOSEPH, master of the doggar Betty of Belfast bound for Stockholm, Sweden, charter party, 1725. [PRONI.D354.388]

BAYLEY, RICHARD, a burgess of Belfast, 1639. [TBB]

BAYLEY, THOMAS, a clothier, was admitted as a Freeman of Belfast in 1639. [TBB]

BEARE, HUMPHREY, a gentleman, was admitted as a Free Stapler of Belfast in 1637. [TBB]

THE PEOPLE OF BELFAST, 1600-1799

BEATTY, DAVID, a weaver, was admitted as a Freeman of Belfast in 1776. [TBB]

BEATTY, FRANCIS, born 1702, died 1765. [Shankill MI, Belfast]

BEATTY, THOMAS, an inn-keeper, was admitted as a Freeman of Belfast in 1726. [TBB]

BEATTY, WILLIAM, a merchant in Belfast, bound for South Carolina in 1766 with indentured servants. [BNL: 29.10.1765]

BECK, THOMAS, a burgess of Belfast, 1642. [TBB]

BECK, THOMAS, a butcher in Belfast, was admitted as a Freeman of Belfast in 1774. [TBB]

BEGGS, HUGH, a shoemaker, was admitted as a Freeman of Belfast in 1728. [TBB]

BEGG, JOHN, a gentleman in Belfast in 1659. [C]

BELL, ANDREW, in Belfast in 1645. [TBB]

BELL, CLEMENT, born 1783, died 1845, husband of Margaret ……., born 1792, died 1827. [Shankill MI, Belfast]

BELL, EDWARD, of Malone, was admitted as a Free Commoner of Belfast, 1645. [TBB]

BELL, HEW, master of the Jean of Belfast 1682-1683. [NRS.E72.20.7; E72.19.8]

BELL, ISAAC, in Belfast, husband of Margaret……., father of John, born 1783, died 1799, George, born 1783, died 1805. [Shankill MI, Belfast]

BELL, ISAAC, born 1776, died 1825, husband of Sarah …., born 1780, died 1834. [Clifton Street MI]

THE PEOPLE OF BELFAST, 1600-1799

BELL, JOHN, in Belfast, 1669. [PRONI.T307A]

BELL, SAMUEL, master of the Charles and Thomas of Belfast 1771. [NRS.E504.4.5]

BELL, THOMAS, a merchant in Belfast, trading with Denmark, a petition, 1677. [TNA.SP63.338.33]

BELL, Captain THOMAS, born 1761, died 1821, husband of Mary ..., born 1759, died 1823. [Clifton Street MI]

BELL, WILLIAM, born 1745, died 1819, husband of Ann ..., born 1746, died 1836.[Clifton Street MI]

BELL, ..., in the barony of Belfast, 1659. [C]

BENNET, JOHN, a cooper, was admitted as a Freeman of Belfast in 1737. [TBB]

BERRY, PIERCE, a laborer, was admitted as a Freeman of Belfast in 1730. [TBB]

BETTY, FRANCIS, a cooper, was admitted as a Freeman of Belfast in 1730. [TBB]

BIGGAR, GEORGE, and his wife Mary, lease of Rosemary Lane, Belfast, 1721. [PRONI.CR3.32.B.1.2]

BIGGAR, JAMES, in Belfast, 1669. [PRONI.T307A]

BIGGAR, JOHN, from Nithsdale in Scotland, to Belfast in 1648. [TBB]

BIGGAR, JOSEPH, master of the Friendship of Belfast trading with Virginia,1700. [TNA.HCAI.26.14]; and his wife Lilias Gall, a deed, 1705. [PRONI.D298.3]

BIGGAR, MICHAEL, from Nithsdale in Scotland to Belfast in 1648, was admitted as a Free Merchant of the Staple of Belfast in 1654, [TBB]; in Belfast, 1669. [PRONI.T307A]; a merchant in Belfast, will subscribed

THE PEOPLE OF BELFAST, 1600-1799

in Edinburgh 1674, refers to his wife Agnes Stewart, and his brother-in-law Thomas Stewart a merchant in Belfast. [TBB]

BIGGAR, MICHAEL, a yeoman in Belfast, a will 1718. [TBB]

BIGGAR, WILLIAM, in Belfast, 1698. [PRONI.D298.2]

BIGGAR, WILLIAM, a carpenter, was admitted as a Freeman of Belfast in 1726. [TBB]

BILE, ANNA, a deed re Rosemary Lane, Belfast, in 1804. [PRONI.CR3.32B.21.2]

BILLINGSBY, HENRY, a gentleman, was admitted as a Freeman of Belfast in 1639. [TBB]

BIRKMYRE, THOMAS, born 1778 in Scotland, died 1846 in Belfast, husband of Catherine….., born 1786 in Scotland, died 1835 in Belfast. [Clifton MI]

BISSET, GEORGE, merchant aboard the Janet of Belfast 1691. [NRS.E72.19.22]

BLACK, GEORGE, a merchant in Belfast, was admitted as a Freeman of Belfast in 1761. [TBB]; will subscribed 1798. [PRONI.T700.1]

BLACK, JOHN, a merchant in Belfast, a bond, 1678. [Kirkcudbright Sheriff Court Records.266]

BLACK, JOHN, co-owner of the Priscilla of Belfast bound for Bremen, Germany, 1720. [PRONI.D354.373]; power of attorney, 1726. [PRONI.D354.615/616]

BLACK, JOHN, a shoemaker, was admitted as a Freeman of Belfast in 1730. [TBB]

BLACK, JOHN, in Belfast, will subscribed 1764. [PRONI.T700.1]

THE PEOPLE OF BELFAST, 1600-1799

BLACK, JOHN, a cabinet maker in Belfast, was admitted as a Freeman of Belfast in 1773. [TBB]

BLACK, ROBERT, a shoemaker, was admitted as a Freeman of Belfast in 1728. [TBB]

BLACK, SAMUEL, a merchant in Belfast, was admitted as a Freeman of Belfast in 1761. [TBB]; in Belfast, a lease, 1770. [PRONI.D509.426]

BLACK, THOMAS, a merchant in Belfast, was admitted as a Freeman of Belfast in 1761. [TBB]

BLACKWOOD, JOHN, a butcher, was admitted as a Freeman of Belfast in 1783. [TBB]

BLACKWOOD, ROBERT, was admitted as a Freeman of Belfast in 1729. [TBB]

BLACKHURST, HENRY, merchant, was admitted as a Free Stapler of Belfast in 1639. [TBB]

BLAINE, JOHN, master of the Diamond of Belfast 1690. [NRS.E72.12.16]; a merchant in Belfast, a deed, 1715. [NRS.RD3.144.507]

BLAIN, WILLIAM, a huckster, was admitted as a Freeman of Belfast in 1730. [TBB]

BLAIR, BRICE, a merchant in Belfast, a deed, 1699. [NRS.RD2.1050]; 1712. [NRS.GD190.3.285.17]

BLAIR, BRICE, a baker in Newton, who had served his apprenticeship in Belfast, was admitted as a Freeman of Belfast in 1748. [TBB]

BLAIR, HENRY, a merchant in Belfast, was admitted as a Freeman of Belfast in 1743. [TBB]

THE PEOPLE OF BELFAST, 1600-1799

BLAIR, JAMES, a preacher, eldest son of Bryce Blair a merchant in Belfast, was admitted as a burgess and guilds-brother of Ayr, 1706. [ABR]

BLAIR, JAMES, in Newtown, a merchant in Belfast, was admitted as a Freeman of Belfast in 1754. [TBB]

BLAKE, WILLIAM, a cook, was admitted as a Freeman of Belfast in 1640. [TBB]

BLAND, NEVILLE, in Belfast, will subscribed 1664. [PRONI.T700.1]

BLAW, JAMES, son of George Blaw of Castlehill [born 1656],'settled as a printer in Belfast, first printer of the Bible in Ireland', partner of Patrick Neill from Glasgow, father of Daniel Blow and Jean Blow, died 1759 in Belfast. [NNQ.VIII.65][SM.21.445][TBB]

BLON, JAMES, a burgess of Belfast, a letter 1754. [PRONI.D354.1007]

BLUETT, SAMUEL, a gentleman in Belfast in 1659. [C]

BODLE, NATHANIEL, of the Falls, was admitted as a Freeman of Belfast in 1758. [TBB]

BODLE, WILLIAM, servant to the Sovereign, was admitted as a Freeman of Belfast in 1758. [TBB]

BOLE, ROBERT, a vintner, was admitted as a Freeman of Belfast in 1725. [TBB]

BOLBY, GAVIN, a burgess of Belfast in 1632, 1639. [TBB]

BOLTON, THOMAS, master of the Nightingale of Belfast 1686. [NRS.E72.19.12]

BOOMER, JAMES, born 1767, died 1820. [Clifton Street MI]

THE PEOPLE OF BELFAST, 1600-1799

BOOMER, MARGARET, born 1755, died 1800. [Shankill MI, Belfast]

BOOTH, HUGH, a smith, was admitted as a Freeman of Belfast in 1639. [TBB]

BOOTH, ROBERT, a wheelwright, was admitted as a Freeman of Belfast in 1635. [TBB]

BORROWFIELD, THOMAS, master of the <u>Christian of Belfast</u> 1774. [NRS.E504.15.24]

BOSKAM, BERNARD, a brazier, was admitted as a Freeman of Belfast in 1643. [TBB]

BOURDOT, NICHOLAS, born 1738 in Chaumont, Bossigni, Champagne, died in Belfast in 1816. [Clifton Street MI]

BOWDEN, JAMES, died 1770. [Shankill MI, Belfast]

BOYCE, JAMES, a merchant, was admitted as a Freeman of Belfast in 1731. [TBB]

BOYD, ALEXANDER, in Belfast, 1669. [PRONI.T307A]

BOYD, ALEXANDER, of the Falls, was admitted as a Freeman of Belfast in 1771. [TBB]

BOYD, BENJAMIN, was admitted as a Freeman of Belfast in 1737. [TBB]

BOYD, GEORGE, a merchant, was admitted as a Freeman of Belfast in 1726. [TBB]

BOYD, HUGH, a merchant in Belfast, 1702. [NRS.GD154.532/533]

BOYD, HUGH, born 1751, died 1815. [Clifton Street MI]

BOYD, JAMES, a tailor, was admitted as a Freeman of 25. [TBB]

THE PEOPLE OF BELFAST, 1600-1799

BOYD, JAMES, a carman, was admitted as a Freeman of Belfast in 1726. [TBB]

BOYD, JAMES, a blacksmith, was admitted as a Freeman of Belfast in 1730. [TBB]

BOYD, JOHN, a burgess of Belfast, 1639. [TBB]; in Belfast, 1669. [PRONI.T307A]; a deed, 1670. [NRS.RD3.66.666]

BOYD, JOHN, master of the <u>Elizabeth of Belfast</u> 1690, [NRS.E72.3.24]; master of the <u>William of Belfast</u> bound for Virginia, 1699. [TNA.CO5.1441]

BOYD, JOHN, a merchant in Belfast, a deposition, 1690. [NRS.GD26.8.84]

BOYD, JOHN, a merchant, was admitted as a Freeman of Belfast in 1730. [TBB]

BOYD, JOHN, in Belfast, a lease on Hanover Quay, Belfast, in 1798. [PRONI.D298.93]

BOYD, NATHANIEL, born 1756, late of Berry Street, Belfast, died 1813, husband of Jane ....., born 1761, died 1831. [Clifton Street MI]

BOYD, PATRICK, an aleseller, was admitted as a Freeman of Belfast in 1730. [TBB]

BOYD, ROBERT, a shoemaker, was admitted as a Freeman of Belfast in 1730. [TBB]

BOYD, ROBERT, a merchant in Belfast. [PRONI.SL19.74]

BOYD, THOMAS, a merchant in Belfast, 1691. [RPCS.XV.69]

BOYLE, or GAW, ANN, wife of John Boyle, an heir of Patrick Gaw in Belfast, 1792. [PRONI.D298.80]

THE PEOPLE OF BELFAST, 1600-1799

BOYLE, JOHN, a weaver, was admitted as a Freeman of Belfast in 1731. [TBB]

BOYLE, JOHN, a co-partner of the Belfast Glass House Company, deed of partnership, 1791. [PRONI.]

BOYLE, ROBERT ARMSTRONG, born in Belfast 1729, a merchant in Kingston, Jamaica, died 1800. [Clifton Street MI]

BRADFORD, JOHN, born 1773, a merchant in Belfast, died 1815. [Clifton Street MI]

BRADFORD, Mrs MARY, born 1777, died 1805, wife of James Bradford. [Shankill MI, Belfast]

BRADLEY, THOMAS, a gentleman, was admitted as a Free Stapler of Belfast in 1637. [TBB]

BRADLEY, Mrs, in Belfast, 1639. [TBB]

BRADSHAW, GEORGE, a merchant, was admitted as a Freeman of Belfast in 1639. [TBB]

BRADSHAW, JOHN, in Belfast, a letter, 1755. [PRONI.D354.649]

BRADSHAW, ROBERT, a merchant, was admitted as a Freeman of Belfast in 1777. [TBB]; a co-partner of the Belfast Glass House Company, deed of partnership, 1791. [PRONI.]

BRADSHAW AND ALEXANDER, merchants in Belfast, 1758. [PRONI.D354.593]

BRAMSTONE, CHARLES, a burgess of Belfast in 1646. [TBB]

BRAMSTONE, THOMAS, a burgess of Belfast in 1632, 1639. [TBB]

THE PEOPLE OF BELFAST, 1600-1799

BRATWHAT, JOHN, was admitted as a Free Commoner of Belfast in 1655. [TBB]

BRAY, ANN, born 1762, daughter of James Bray, steward of the Belfast Poor House, died 1788. [Shankill MI, Belfast]

BRETLAND, THOMAS, an adventurer who was granted land in the south-east quarter of the barony of Belfast, 1643. [SPI.1642-1659: 354]

BRETT, CHARLES, a co-partner of the Belfast Glass House Company, deed of partnership, 1791. [PRONI.]

BRICE, Captain EDWARD, was admitted as a burgess of Belfast in 1697. [TBB]; a merchant burgess, died 1707. [BMF]

BRICE, EDWARD, in Belfast, will subscribed 1738. [PRONI.T700.1]; probate 1741. [NAI.T5127]

BRICE, ROBERT, a clerk, was admitted as a Free Commoner of Belfast in 1652. [TBB]

BRISTOW, Mrs DOROTHY, wife of Charles Bristow of Antrim, died in Belfast in 1766. [FDJ.4074]

BRISTOW, Reverend WILLIAM, vicar of Belfast Corporation Church in 1772. [TBB]

BRITTEN, JOHN, a sawyer from Belfast, in Glasgow by 1818. [NRS.AD14.18.67]

BRITTEN, Mrs MARTHA, born 1783, wife of Alexander Britten, died 1817. [Clifton Street MI][New Burying Ground MI]

BRITTEN, WILLIAM, born 1775, died 1815. [Clifton Street MI][New Burying Ground MI].

THE PEOPLE OF BELFAST, 1600-1799

BROOKS, JOHN, a glazier, was admitted as a Freeman of Belfast in 1752. [TBB]

BROWN, or STEWART, ELINOR, in Belfast, will subscribed 1784. [PRONI.T700.1]

BROWN, HUGH, master of the <u>Recovery of Belfast</u> which was shipwrecked when bound for Charleston, South Carolina, in 1793. [NRS.AC7.66][BNL]

BROWN, JAMES, a merchant in Dublin, was admitted as a Freeman of Belfast in 1753. [TBB]

BROWN, JAMES, born 1766, died 1797. [Shankill MI, Belfast]

BROWN, JOHN, a merchant, was admitted as a Freeman of Belfast in 1642. [TBB]

BROWN, JOHN, in Belfast, a lease, 1686. [PRONI.D509.29]

BROWN, JOHN, a seaman from Belfast, to be released from Edinburgh or Canongate tollbooths in 1689, [RPCS.XIII.554]

BROWN, JOHN, a chapman, was admitted as a Freeman of Belfast in 1730. [TBB]

BROWN, JOHN, in Petershill, Belfast, a mortgage, 1775. [PRONI.D509.662]; letters and papers from 1773. [NRS.GD200/18]

BROWN, JOHN, a banker in Belfast, 1787. [TBB]

BROWN, JOHN, Sovereign of Belfast in 1796. [TBB]

BROWN, NEILL, born 1723, settled in Chester County, Pennsylvania, in 1765, a Loyalist, returned to Belfast by 1788. [TNA.AO12.102.135]

THE PEOPLE OF BELFAST, 1600-1799

BROWN, PAUL, was admitted as a Freeman of Belfast in 1783. [TBB]

BROWN, ROBERT, master of the Anna Helena of Belfast 1689. [NRS.E72.12.14]

BROWN, SAMUEL, a merchant in Belfast, was admitted as a Freeman of Belfast in 1774. [TBB]; a conveyance of premises in Skipper's Lane, Belfast, 1781; [PRONI.D238.53/56]

BROWN, THOMAS, was admitted as a Freeman of Belfast in 1777. [TBB]; a co-partner of the Belfast Glass House Company, deed of partnership, 1791. [PRONI.]

BROWN, WILLIAM, born 1658 in Belfast, son of John Brown, who after serving as an officer in the army, settled at Clonboy in 1691. [LGI.74]

BROWNE, WILLIAM, was admitted as a Freeman of Belfast in 1727. [TBB]

BROWN, WILLIAM, a merchant in Dublin, was admitted as a Freeman of Belfast in 1753. [TBB]

BROWN, WILLIAM, born 1774, died 1814, husband of Abigail. [New Burying Ground MI]

BROWN, WILLIAM, born 1790 in Belfast, naturalised in New York, 1811.

BRUEN, JOHN, a tailor in Belfast, was admitted as a Freeman of Belfast in 1754. [TBB]

BRYAN, WILLIAM, in Belfast in 1645. [TBB]

BRUCE, ROBERT, a barber, was admitted as a Freeman of Belfast in 1727. [TBB]

THE PEOPLE OF BELFAST, 1600-1799

BRUCE, THOMAS, in Belfast, was apprenticed for 5 years aboard the Isaac of Belfast in 1730. [PRONI.D354.394]

BUCHANAN, JOHN, a merchant in Belfast, probate 1784, Dublin

BULLER, JAMES, a tanner burgess of Belfast from 1690 to 1703. [BMF]

BULLOCK, ABELL, a smith, was admitted as a Freeman of Belfast in 1729. [TBB]

BULLICK, GEORGE, born 1758, died 1822, husband of Isabella, born 1755, died 1822. [New Burying Ground MI]

BUNTIN, ARTHUR, a merchant in Belfast, was admitted as a Freeman of Belfast in 1760. [TBB]; in Belfast, a lease in 1770. [PRONI.D509.442]

BURK, WILLIAM, a mealman, was admitted as a Free Commoner of Belfast in 1654. [TBB]

BURLEIGH, JOHN, a merchant, was admitted as a Freeman of Belfast in 1731. [TBB]

BURN, CHARLES, a cooper, was admitted as a Freeman of Belfast in 1726. [TBB]

BURNS, JAMES, a butcher in Belfast, was admitted as a Freeman of Belfast in 1760. [TBB]

BURNS, TIMOTHY, a vinter in Belfast, was admitted as a Freeman of Belfast in 1760. [TBB]

BURNES, ..., in the barony of Belfast, 1659. [C]

BURT, WILLIAM, a slater, was admitted as a Freeman of Belfast in 1726. [TBB]

THE PEOPLE OF BELFAST, 1600-1799

BURTON, BENJAMIN, of Burtonhall, was admitted as a Freeman of Belfast in 1754. [TBB]

BURTON, THOMAS, a shoemaker, was admitted as a Freeman of Belfast in 1638. [TBB]

BUTLE, DAVID, a merchant in Belfast, a letter book, 1696-1703. [PRONI.D1449]; a merchant burgess, died 1707. [BMF]

BYRES, ROBERT, master of the <u>Bettie of Belfast</u> 1707. [ACA.APB.2]

BYRES, ……, master of the <u>Sara of Belfast</u> 1721. [NRS.AC9.757]

BYRN, NATHANIEL, a burgess, 1707. [BMF]

BYRTT, ARTHUR, a burgess of Belfast, a letter 1754. [PRONI.D354.1007]; Sovereign of Belfast in 1744. [TBB]

BYRTT, NATHANIEL, in Carrickfergus, was admitted as a Freeman of Belfast in 1737. [TBB]

BYRTT, ROBERT, the Sovereign of Belfast, 1737. [PRONI.D354.1011]

BYRTT, WILLIAM, died 1788, husband of Juliana ……, born 1761, died 1801, parents of William Byrtt, born 1786, late surgeon of the 24th Regiment, died 1845 in Belfast. [New Burying Ground MI]

CAHAN, THOMAS, a cooper in Belfast, was admitted as a Freeman of Belfast in 1737. [TBB]

CALDER, JOHN, a weaver and rioter in Belfast, 1614. [OB.38]

CALDWELL, JOHN, master of the <u>Ross of Belfast</u> 1689, [NRS.E72.3.21]; master of the <u>St Andrew of Belfast</u> 1691. [NRS.E72.19.21]; master of the <u>Friendship of Belfast</u>

THE PEOPLE OF BELFAST, 1600-1799

from Virginia to Liverpool in 1700, [TNA.CO5.1311]; from Belfast to Charleston, South Carolina. in 1718. [PRONI.354.370]

CALDWELL, JOHN, born 1732, died 1785, wife Jane ....., born 1728, died 1785. [Shankill MI, Belfast]; a lease in Carrickfergus Street, Belfast, 1778. [PRONI.D298.46]

CALWELL, Ensign JAMES, in Belfast in 1684. [SPDom.1684.259]

CALWELL, JAMES, a book-keeper, late of Belfast, 1684. [SPDom.1684.259]

CALLWELL, JOHN, in Belfast, a lease, 1747. [PRONI.D298.14]

CALWELL, JOHN, of Springfield, born 1758, died 1800. [Shankill MI, Belfast]

CAMPBELL, ANDREW, a shoemaker, was admitted as a Freeman of Belfast in 1730. [TBB]

CAMPBELL, DOUGALL, in Belfast 1699, son of Alexander Campbell a merchant in Edinburgh, a letter. [NRS.RH15.9.14/67]

CAMPBELL HUGH, a merchant, was admitted as a Free Commoner of Belfast in 1650. [TBB]

CAMPBELL, JAMES, a merchant, was admitted as a Free Commoner of Belfast in 1651. [TBB]

CAMPBELL, JOHN, in Belfast, 1669. [PRONI.1307A]

CAMPBELL, JOHN, a merchant in Belfast, a letter, 1756. [PRONI.D354.781]; a merchant in Belfast, was admitted as a Freeman of Belfast in 1760. [TBB]

CAMPBELL, JOHN, master of the Ranger of Belfast 1772. [NRS.E504.8.5]

THE PEOPLE OF BELFAST, 1600-1799

CAMPBELL, JOHN, in Belfast, a lease in 1780. [PRONI.D509.614]

CAMPBELL, MARGARET, relict of James Muir a shipmaster in Belfast, petitioned the Privy Council of Scotland in 1690. [RPCS.XV.413]

CAMPBELL, WILLIAM, born 1776, of Belfast, died 1814. [New Burying Ground MI]

CAMPBELL and DONALDSON, vintners in Belfast, 1766. [PRONI.D207.19.111]

CAMPBELL, ..., in the barony of Belfast, 1659. [C]

CARLILE, WILLIAM, died 1762. [Shankill MI, Belfast]

CARMICHAEL, JOHN, in Belfast, 1669. [PRONI.T307A]

CARMICHAEL, JOHN, in Belfast, a lease in 1770. [PRONI.D509.446]

CARMICHAEL, Reverend WILLIAM, born 1729, Pastor of the Seceding Congregation of Belfast, died 1798. [Shankill MI, Belfast][PRONI.CR3.32.B.1.9]

CARMICHAEL, WILLIAM, a cooper, was admitted as a Freeman of Belfast in 1725. [TBB]

CARNES, ADAM, was admitted as a Free Commoner and Staple Merchant of Belfast in 1653. [TBB]

CARNAHAN, JOHN, a shopkeeper, was admitted as a Freeman of Belfast in 1725. [TBB]

CARPENTER, JOHN, a burgess, 1717. [BMF]

CARR, JAMES, a tailor, was admitted as a Freeman of Belfast in 1638. [TBB]

CARR, THOMAS, a cooper, was admitted as a Free Commoner of Belfast in 1650. [TBB]

THE PEOPLE OF BELFAST, 1600-1799

CARRON, RICHARD, a weaver in Belfast, was admitted as a Freeman of Belfast in 1638. [TBB]; in Belfast in 1645. [TBB]

CARRON, THOMAS, constable of Belfast in 1646, [TBB]; in Belfast, a lease, 1656. [PRONI.D509.13]

CARSON, JAMES, a tailor, was admitted as a Freeman of Belfast in 1752. [TBB]; a lease of Peter's Hill, Belfast, in 1770. [PRONI.D509.448]

CARSON, SAMUEL, was admitted as a Freeman of Belfast in 1744. [TBB]

CARSON, SAMUEL, born 1770, a merchant from Belfast, was naturalised in South Carolina in 1804.[NARA.M1183]

CARSON, WILLIAM, born 1722, died 1735, [Shankill MI, Belfast]

CARSWELL, JOSEPH, a mariner, was admitted as a Freeman of Belfast in 1726. [TBB]; master of the James and Ellice at Gibraltar, 1731. [PRONI.D354.1484/2]

CARTER, ALICE, lease of Carrickhill, Belfast, 1792. [PRONI.D298.78]

CARTWRIGHT, JOHN, a farmer in Malone, was admitted as a Freeman of Belfast in 1746. [TBB]

CARTWRIGHT, THOMAS, son of John Cartwright farmer in Malone, was admitted as a Freeman of Belfast in 1746. [TBB]

CARTWRIGHT, WILLIAM, son of John Cartwright farmer in Malone, was admitted as a Freeman of Belfast in 1746. [TBB]

CARUTH, WALTER, a chapman, was admitted as a Free Stapler of Belfast in 1644. [TBB]

THE PEOPLE OF BELFAST, 1600-1799

CATHERWOOD, QUINTIN, a burgess of Belfast, 1639. [TBB]; in Belfast, 1643. [TBB]; a Scot in Belfast, to be transported to the west of Ireland in 1653. [TBB]

CATHERWOOD, SAMUEL, a merchant, was admitted as a Freeman of Belfast in 1730. [TBB]

CATHERWOOD, WILLIAM, master of the Isaac of Belfast bound for Sweden, charter party, 1726. [PRONI.D354.389]

CAUGHEY, JOHN, in Belfast, a conveyance of a tenement in Ann Street, Belfast, 1795. [PRONI.D199.20]

CAULFIELD, ROBERT, a shoemaker, was admitted as a Freeman of Belfast in 1729. [TBB]

CHADS, HENRY, a merchant in Belfast ca1689, [PRONI.T559.15.133]; petitioned the Privy Council of Scotland regarding munitions which he had purchased, stored in Ayr and were bound for northern Ireland, in 1689. [RPCS.XIII.537]; a ruling elder from Belfast, at the Synod of Ulster in 1692. [GSU.7]; Probate, 1711.

CHALMERS, ALEXANDER, a merchant in Belfast, a deed, 1729. [NRS.SC20.33.11]

CHALMERS, DAVID, senior, a merchant in Belfast, was admitted as a burgess and guilds-brother of Ayr in 1697. [ABR]

CHALMERS, DAVID, junior, a merchant in Belfast, was admitted as a burgess and guilds-brother of Ayr in 1696. [ABR]

CHALMERS, JAMES, a merchant in Belfast, was admitted as a burgess and guilds-brother of Ayr, 1665, [ABR]

THE PEOPLE OF BELFAST, 1600-1799

CHALMERS, JAMES, a merchant in Belfast, husband of Helen Kennedy, a bond, 1671. [NRS.RD2.30.319]

CHALMERS, JAMES, a merchant, was admitted as a Freeman of Belfast in 1725. [TBB]

CHALMERS, JAMES, a merchant, in Antigua, a letter, 1731. [PRONI.D162.24]

CHALMERS, JOHN, was admitted as a Freeman of Belfast in 1693. [TBB]

CHALMERS, WILLIAM, a merchant, was admitted as a Freeman of Belfast in 1728. [TBB]

CHAMBERS, JAMES, in Belfast, 1669. [PRONI.T307A]; in Belfast, will subscribed 1681. [PRONI.T700.1]

CHAMBERS, JAMES, a merchant in Belfast, a deed 1714. [NRS.RD4.114.49]

CHAPMAN, JAMES, master of the Joan of Belfast 1681. [NRS.E72.19.5] CHALMERS, JOHN, a merchant burgess, died in 1708. [BMF]

CHAPMAN, ST JOHN, in Belfast, a lease, 1770. [PRONI.D509.440]

CHARLES, THOMAS, a butcher, was admitted as a Freeman of Belfast in 1639. [TBB]

CHARLEY, JOHN, was admitted as a Freeman of Belfast in 1729. [TBB]

CHARLY, RALPH, in Belfast, a deed, 1724. [PRONI.D389.15]

CHARLY, WILLIAM, the water bailiff of Belfast, 1738, [PRONI.D354.1011]; in Belfast, probate 1744, Connor. [PRONI.D272.71]

THE PEOPLE OF BELFAST, 1600-1799

CHERRY, Dr MOSES, was admitted as a Freeman of Belfast in 1725. [TBB]

CHICHESTER, CHARLES, in Belfast, 1699. [PRONI.D778.27]; a gentleman burgess 1697-1701. [BMF]

CHICHESTER, ARTHUR, Governor of Belfast Castle in 1603, 1604. [PRONI.D509/2; T956/4]; Earl of Belfast, probate 1625, PCC

CHICHESTER, SIMON, MA, vicar of Belfast Corporation Church in 1632.

CHRISTOPHERSON, RICHARD, a butcher, was admitted as a Freeman of Belfast in 1639. [TBB]

CHRISTIAN, ISRAEL, a lease of Castle Street, Belfast, 1670. [PRONI.D508.22]

CHRISTIE, JOHN, in Belfast, 1669. [PRONI.T307A]

CHRUCHLEY, JOHN, a plasterer, was admitted as a burgess of Belfast in 1651. [TBB]

CHUDLEIGH, THOMAS, in Belfast, 1635. [TBB]

CLARK, ANDREW, born 1702, died 1742. [Shankill MI]

CLARK, FRANCIS, in Belfast, a lease of Old Park in Belfast, 1777. [PRONI.D509.579]

CLARK, JAMES, a merchant in Belfast, was admitted as a Freeman of Belfast in 1733. [TBB]; an account, 1740. [PRONI.D354.522/524]

CLARK, JOHN, a pattern-maker, was admitted as a Freeman of Belfast in 1730. [TBB]

THE PEOPLE OF BELFAST, 1600-1799

CLARKE, RALPH, an adventurer who was granted land in the north-east quarter of the barony of Belfast, 1643. [SPI.1642-1659: 354]

CLEMENTS, EDWARD, a burgess, 1715. [BMF]

CLEMENTS, JAMES, master of the Draper of Belfast in 1774. [NRS.E504.15.24]

CLOGH, JAMES, was admitted as a Freeman of Belfast in 1641. [TBB]

CLUGSTON, JOHN, a merchant, was admitted as a Free Stapler of Belfast in 1643. [TBB]; a gentleman in Belfast, 1659. [C]

CLUGSTON, JOHN, a burgess 1721. [BMF]; Sovereign of Belfast in 1726. [TBB]

CLUGSTON, MICHAEL, a merchant in Belfast, a bond, 1677, [NRS.RD2.43.334]; a deed, 1682. [NRS.RD4.50.358]

CLUGSTON, ROBERT, was admitted as a Freeman of Belfast in 1645, [TBB]; a Scot in Belfast, to be transported to the west of Ireland in 1653. [TBB]; a merchant in Belfast, a deed, 1682. [NRS.RD4.51.162]

CLUGGESTON, WILLIAM, was admitted as a Freeman of Belfast, 1638. [TSB]; a gentleman in Belfast in 1659. [C]

CLUGSTON, WILLIAM, apprentice to Henry Duncan an apothecary, was admitted as a Freeman of Belfast in 1730. [TBB]

COATS, ADAM, of the Falls, was admitted as a Freeman of Belfast in 1771. [TBB]

COATS, JAMES, in the Liberties of Belfast, 1669. [PRONI.T307A]

THE PEOPLE OF BELFAST, 1600-1799

COATS, JOHN, in Belfast, a lease, 1770. [PRONI.D509.450]; of the Falls, was admitted as a Freeman of Belfast in 1771. [TBB]

COATS, PHILLIP, of the Falls, was admitted as a Freeman of Belfast in 1737. [TBB]

COATS, PHILIP, born 1762, died 1828. [Shankill MI, Belfast]

COATS, WHITESIDE, of the Falls, was admitted as a Freeman of Belfast in 1771. [TBB]

COATS, ROSE, born 1729, died 1814. [Shankill MI, Belfast]

COATS, VICTOR, in Belfast, a deed, 1796. [PRONI.D447.20]

COATS, WILLIAM, in the Liberties of Belfast, 1669. [PRONI.T307A]

COATS, WILLIAM, of the Falls and the townland of Ballymurchy, was admitted as a Freeman of Belfast in 1748. [TBB]

COATS, WILLIAM, of the Falls, was admitted as a Freeman of Belfast in 1771. [TBB]

COCHRANE, ADAM, a merchant on board the _James and Robert of Belfast_ 1696. [NRS.E72.19.23]

COCHRAN, HUGH, a tailor, was admitted as a Freeman of Belfast in 1725. [TBB]

COFFIN, ROBERT, a smith, was admitted as a Freeman of Belfast in 1726. [TBB]

COLEMAN, JOHN, a merchant, was admitted as a Freeman of Belfast in 1726. [TBB]; a merchant in

THE PEOPLE OF BELFAST, 1600-1799

Belfast, was admitted as a burgess and guilds-brother of Ayr in 1730. [ABR]

COLEMAN, RICHARD, a yarn merchant, was admitted as a Freeman of Belfast in 1730. [TBB]

COLEMAN, ROBERT, born 1795, a mariner from Belfast, was naturalised in South Carolina in 1818.[NARA.M1183]

COLLYER, THOMAS, was admitted as a Freeman of Belfast in 1727. [TBB]

COLQUIN, FRANCIS, in Belfast, a lease, 1770. [PRONI.D509.453]

CONNELL, CHARLES and Sons, merchants in Belfast, a letter, 1800. [NRS.GD260.2.31]

CONNOLLY, JAMES, in Belfast, a letter, 1804. [NRS.GD112.52.601]

CONNOR, or GAW, ELIZABETH, an heir of Patrick Gaw in Belfast, 1792. [PRONI.D298.80]

CONYNGHAM, SAMUEL, in Belfast and Barbados, will subscribed 1783. [PRONI.T700.1]

CONYNGHAM, SAMUEL, in Belfast, will subscribed 1785. [PRONI.T700.1]

CONYNGHAM, THOMAS, a merchant in Belfast, was admitted as a burgess and guilds-brother of Ayr in 1750. [ABR]

CONYNGHAM, WEDDELL, in Belfast, will subscribed 1798. [PRONI.T700.1]

COOK, EDWARD, master of the <u>Antelope of Belfast,</u> trading with Philadelphia, 1682. [HSPa][PMHB.8/9][NB the Antelope of Belfast also arrived in the James River, Virginia, in 1679]

THE PEOPLE OF BELFAST, 1600-1799

COOK, THOMAS, in Belfast in 1645. [TBB]

COOTE, Sir CHARLES, was admitted as a Free Stapler of Belfast in 1640. [TBB]

CORBETT, ALLAN, a merchant in Belfast, 1683. [NRS.RH15.91.60]

CORBETT, JOSEPH, master of the James of Belfast in 1749. [NRS.E504.4.1]

CORBETT, ROBERT, a shoemaker, was admitted as a Freeman of Belfast in 1730. [TBB]

CORBETT, THOMAS, in Belfast, 1669. [PRONI.T307A]

CORDINER, WILLIAM, a merchant, was admitted as a Free Commoner of Belfast in 1647. [TBB]

CORNER, WILLIAM, in Belfast in 1645. [TBB]

CORNWALL, JOHN, school-master of Belfast, ca.1650. [TBB]

CORRY, JOHN, was admitted as a Free Commoner of Belfast, in 1654. [TBB]

CORSON, JOHN, master of the James of Belfast 1672, 1673. [NRS.E72.20.3/4]

COSGROVE, DANIEL, in Belfast, a lease, 1770. [PRONI.D509.454]

COSHNAN, PHELOMY, town sergeant of Belfast, 1640. [TBB]

COTTER, JOHN, a clothier, was admitted as a Freeman of Belfast in 1639. [TBB]

COTTER, JOHN, in Belfast, lease of Mill Street, Belfast, 1727. [PRONI.D509.49]

THE PEOPLE OF BELFAST, 1600-1799

COTTER, WILLIAM, in Belfast, 1669. [PRONI.T307A]

COULTER, NATHANIEL, born 1757, died 1828, husband of Margaret ....., born 1753, died 1834. [Shankill MI, Belfast]

COULTER, THOMAS, a tailor, was admitted as a Freeman of Belfast in 1731. [TBB]

COUPLAND, JOHN, was admitted as a Freeman of Belfast, 1644. [TBB.2249]

COWAN, JOHN, a merchant aboard the <u>Content of Belfast</u> trading with France in 1681. [SPDom.1681.228/280]

COWAN, ..., in the barony of Belfast, 1659. [C]

CRACKEN, WILLIAM, a tailor and Freeman of Belfast in 1673. [TBB]

CRAFORD, JAMES, a farmer, was admitted as a Freeman of Belfast in 1728. [TBB]

CRAFORD, JOHN, a farmer, was admitted as a Freeman of Belfast in 1728. [TBB]

CRAFORD, MATTHEW, a huckster, was admitted as a Freeman of Belfast in 1728. [TBB]

CRAFFORD, WILLIAM, a merchant who was admitted as a burgess of Belfast in 1686, [TBB.153]; in Belfast, a lease, 1688. [PRONI.D412.1]; Sovereign of Belfast, present at the Synod of Ulster in Antrim, 1697. [GSU.15]; will, probate 11 October 1716 in Dublin. It refers to his wife Janet, his only son David, grandson William Crafford, grand-daughter Ann Crafford, daughter Helenor wife of Roger Haddock, sister Grissell McCologh, George McCartney in Belfast, Reverend John Kirkpatrick, Robert Donaldson an attorney, Robert

THE PEOPLE OF BELFAST, 1600-1799

Stevenson, Hugh Moore, witnesses John Chalmers and Benjamin Patterson merchants, and William King servant to Samuel McClinton an innkeeper, all in Belfast.

CRAIG, GABRIEL, master of the Elizabeth of Belfast 1695. [NRS.E72.19.23]

CRAIG, ROBERT, in Belfast, a bond, 1718. [PRONI.D354.366/367]

CRAIG, ..., in the barony of Belfast, 1659. [C]

CRANFORD, ROBERT, a merchant aboard the Rose of Belfast 1691. [NRS.E72.12.18]

CRANSTON, Lieutenant THOMAS, a Scot in Belfast, to be transported to the west of Ireland in 1653. [TBB]

CRAWFORD, ARTHUR, born 1790, a merchant in Belfast, died 1873. [Shankill MI, Belfast]

CRAWFORD, CHARLES, in Belfast, will subscribed 1769. [PRONI.T700.1]

CRAWFORD, DANIEL, in Belfast, will subscribed 1789. [PRONI.T700.1]

CRAWFORD, DAVID, in Belfast, will subscribed 1737. [PRONI.T700.1]

CRAWFORD, JAMES, master of the Batchelor of Belfast was admitted as a burgess and guilds-brother of Ayr, 1725. [ABR]

CRAWFORD, JAMES, a merchant, was admitted as a Freeman of Belfast in 1753. [TBB]

CRAWFORD, JOHN, in the Liberties of Belfast, 1669. [PRONI.T307A]

THE PEOPLE OF BELFAST, 1600-1799

CRAWFORD, JOHN, born 1758, in Belfast, died 1830. [Shankill MI, Belfast]

CRAWFORD, OWEN, in the Liberties of Belfast, 1669. [PRONI.T307A]

CRAWFORD, THOMAS, in the Liberties of Belfast, 1669. [PRONI.T307A]

CRAWFORD, THOMAS, in Belfast, a deed, 1692. [PRONI.D509.31]

CRAWFORD, WALTER, in Belfast, a lease in Union Street, Belfast, in 1796. [PRONI.D438.4]

CRAWFORD, WILLIAM, was admitted as a burgess of Belfast in 1686. [TBB]; died 1707. [BMF]

CRAWFORD, WILLIAM, a merchant and Member of Parliament for Belfast in the Irish Parliament in 1703, 1707. [TBB]

CRAWFORD, Mrs, wife of James Crawford, died in Belfast in 1766. [FDJ. 4082]

CREIGHTON, WILLIAM, in Belfast, 1669. [PRONI.T307A]

CROMBIE, HUGH, born 1781, a merchant from Belfast, was naturalised in South Carolina in 1804.[NARA.M1183]

CROMBIE, JOSEPH, born 1778, a merchant from Belfast, was naturalised in South Carolina in 1804.[NARA.M1183]

CROMEY, FRANCIS, a merchant, was admitted as a Freeman of Belfast in 1725. [TBB]

CROSSIN, WILLIAM, in Belfast, a lease in Gregg's Land, Belfast, 1792. [PRONI.D491.54]

THE PEOPLE OF BELFAST, 1600-1799

CRUMBLE, WATERHOUSE, a burgess of Belfast in 1642. [TBB]

CRUTCHLEY, PAUL, a currier, was admitted as a Freeman of Belfast in 1728. [TBB]

CUDBERT, JOHN, a merchant, was admitted as a Freeman of Belfast in 1728. [TBB]

CULBERT, JOHN, a merchant, was admitted as a Freeman of Belfast in 1728. [TBB]

CULTON, JOHN, born 1743, died 1817, husband of Catherine ...., born 1761, did 1837. [Shankill MI, Belfast]

CUMIN, ANN, born 1746, died 1802. [Shankill MI, Belfast]

CUNNINGHAM, CHARLES, a merchant in Belfast, was admitted as a Freeman of Belfast in 1760. [TBB]

CUNNINGHAM, JOHN, in Belfast in 1645. [TBB]

CUNNINGHAM, JOHN, a carman, was admitted as a Freeman of Belfast in 1728. [TBB]

CUNNINGHAM, JOHN, born 1752, died 1815, husband of Elizabeth ....., born 1757, died 1812. [Shankill MI, Belfast]; a co-partner of the Belfast Glass House Company, deed of partnership, 1791. [PRONI.]

CUNNINGHAM, JOHN, from Belfast to Boston, a journal 1795-1796. [PRONI.D394.1]

CUNNINGHAM, Mrs MARGARET, born 1711, wife of Alexander Cunningham a merchant in Belfast, died 1780. [Shankill MI, Belfast]

CUNNINGHAM, THOMAS, was admitted as a Freeman of Belfast, 1638. [TBB.246]; a merchant, sometime in

THE PEOPLE OF BELFAST, 1600-1799

Belfast, was admitted as a burgess and guilds-brother of Ayr in 1650. [ABR]

CUNNINGHAM, WADDEL, merchant in Belfast, was admitted as a Freeman of Belfast in 1773. [TBB]; a lease in the High Street of Belfast, 1770. [PRONI.D199.4]; MP for Carrickfergus in 1783, a partner in the bank Cunningham, Rankin, Brown and Campbell in Belfast in 1784, died 1797 in Belfast. [EWJ.1]

CURRY, DANIEL, was admitted as a Freeman of Belfast in 1783. [TBB]

CURRY, JAMES, in Belfast, a lease, 1737. [PRONI.D389.16]

CURRY, JASPER, a merchant in Belfast, was admitted as a Freeman of Belfast in 1760. [TBB]

CURRY, SAMUEL, a shopkeeper, was admitted as a Freeman of Belfast in 1725. [TBB]

CURRY, THOMAS, in Hollywood, was admitted as a Freeman of Belfast in 1728. [TBB]

CUTHBERT, JOSEPH, born 1762 in Belfast, naturalised in New York, 1802.

DAM, EDWARD, a butcher, was admitted as a Free Commoner of Belfast in 1649. [TBB]

DAVENPORT, FRANCIS, a merchant in Belfast, 1720, a witness to the will of Richard Hodgkinson probate 1720 Dublin.

DAVIDSON, ALEXANDER, master of the <u>Jane and Mary of Belfast</u> 1716. [NRS.E508.10.6]

DAVIDSON, JOHN, lease of Graham's Entry, Belfast, in 1793. [PRONI.D298.82A]

THE PEOPLE OF BELFAST, 1600-1799

DAVIE, WILLIAM, master of the Prosperity of Belfast trading with the Canary Islands in 1690. [NRS.E72.3.20]

DAVIES, JOHN, a gentleman, merchant, and burgess of Belfast from 1642 until 1667. [TBB][BMF]

DAVIES, NATHANIEL, master of the ketch Fullwood of Belfast 1682. [NRS.E72.19.6]

DAVIES, WILLIAM, was admitted as a Freeman of Belfast in 1643. [TBB]

DAVIES, WILLIAM, born 1676 in Belfast, a four year indentured servant, emigrated via Liverpool aboard the Elizabeth and Ann, master William Benn, bound for Montserrat in 1700. [LRO]

DAVISON, ANDREW, of Tullnagee, was admitted as a Freeman of Belfast in 1747. [TBB]

DAVISON, JOHN, master of the Swan of Belfast 1680s. [NRS.E72.6.25]

DAVISON, JAMES, a tailor, was admitted as a Freeman of Belfast in 1725. [TBB]

DAVISON, MATTHEW, a yeoman in Belfast, witness to the will of James Smith, probate 1720, Dublin.

DAWSON, THOMAS, a joiner, was admitted as a Free Commoner of Belfast in 1654. [TBB]

DAWSON, WILLIAM, father of James Dawson, born 1761, died 1762, and Sarah Dawson, born 1748, died 1763. [Shankill MI, Belfast]

DAYLEY, JOHN, a butcher, was admitted as a Freeman of Belfast in 1728. [TBB]

DEAKE, HUGH, a gentleman in Belfast in 1659. [C]

THE PEOPLE OF BELFAST, 1600-1799

DELAP, ROBERT, in Belfast, 1805. [PRONI.D207.67]

DENMAN, EDWARD, a merchant, was admitted as a Free Commoner and Staple Merchant of Belfast in 1655. [TBB]

DENNIS, PHILIP, of the Falls, was admitted as a Freeman of Belfast in 1771. [TBB]

DICK, THOMAS, master of the ……..of Belfast in 1685. [NRS.E72.20.13]

DICKEY, ROBERT, a cordiner, was admitted as a Freeman of Belfast in 1731. [TBB]

DICKSON, JOHN, a Free Stapler of Belfast, 1635. [TBB]

DICKSON, RICHARD, in Belfast, a lease, 1787. [PRONI.D199.18]; lease in Castle Street, Belfast, 1794. [PRONI.D199.18]

DIGBY, ESSEX, a preacher in Belfast in 1651. [TBB]

DIGHTON, RALPH, a burgess of Belfast, 1639. [TBB]; town constable of Belfast, 1640. [TBB]

DILLON, Sir JAMES, was admitted as a Free Stapler of Belfast in 1640. [TBB]

DINGLEY, JOSEPH, a tailor, was admitted as a Freeman of Belfast in 1728. [TBB]

DIXON, SAMUEL, in Cook's Court, Belfast, a letter, 1754. [PRONI.D354.318]

DOAKE, HUGH, a gentleman, was admitted as a burgess of Belfast in 1645. [TBB]; a Scot in Belfast, to be transported to the west of Ireland in 1653. [TBB]; a burgess 1645 -1669. [BMF]

THE PEOPLE OF BELFAST, 1600-1799

DOAKE, JOHN, a husbandman, was admitted as a Free Commoner of Belfast in 1647. [TBB]

DOAKE, THOMAS, in Belfast, 1643. [TBB]

DOBBIN, Dr JAMES, in Belfast, a letter, 1754. [PRONI.D354.324]; a burgess of Belfast, a letter 1754. [PRONI.D354.1007]

DOBBIN, JOHN, was admitted as a Freeman of Belfast in 1752. [TBB]

DOBBIN, RIGBY, was admitted as a Freeman of Belfast in 1752. [TBB]

DOBBIN, Captain WILLIAM, born 1650, a merchant in Belfast, died 1723. [PRONI.T367]; Deputy Collector at the port of Belfast in 1670. [NLI.ms8110]

DOHERTY, HUGH, born 1774, died 1818. [Shankill MI, Belfast]

DOLLAR, ROBERT, of Belfast, born 1771, died 1820. [Shankill MI, Belfast]

DONALDSON, ALEXANDER, in Belfast, will subscribed 1774. [PRONI.T700.1]

DONALDSON, ARCHIBALD, in Belfast, will subscribed 1773. [PRONI.T700.1]

DONALDSON, HUGH, in Belfast, will subscribed 1762. [PRONI.T700.1]

DONALDSON, MATTHEW, a burgess of Belfast, a letter 1754. [PRONI.D354.1007]

DONALDSON, ..., in the barony of Belfast, 1659. [C]

DONLEVY, HENRY, was admitted as a Freeman of Belfast in 1729. [TBB]

THE PEOPLE OF BELFAST, 1600-1799

DONVILL, WILLIAM, in Belfast, born 1712, died 1795. [Shankill MI, Belfast]

DOOGAN, ROBERT, a tailor, was admitted as a Freeman of Belfast in 1730. [TBB]

DORMAN, JOHN, a mealmonger in Belfast, was admitted as a Freeman of Belfast in 1754. [TBB]

DORNAN, JOHN, servant to Isaac McCartney, was admitted as a Freeman of Belfast in 1730. [TBB]

DOUGALL, ANDREW, born 1777, died 1817. [Shankill MI, Belfast]

DOUEY, JAMES, in Belfast in 1645. [TBB]

DOULE, JOHN, a carman, was admitted as a Freeman of Belfast in 1725. [TBB]

DOWNES, LEWIS, DD, vicar of Belfast Corporation Church in 1642.

DOWNMAN, WILLIAM, was admitted as a Freeman of Belfast in 1641. [TBB]

DOWNEY, JOHN, was admitted as a Freeman of Belfast in 1742. [TBB]

DRENNAN, Mrs ANN, a widow in Belfast, a lease, 1783. [PRONI.D270.11]; in Donegal Street, Belfast, a will, 1790. [PRONI.D270.16]

DRENAN, JOHN, a lease in Schoolhouse Lane, Belfast, 1670. [PRONI.D509.25]

DUFF, JOHN, in Belfast, sovereign there in 1746, [TBB]; a will, 1753. [PRONI.D1255.3.32A][NAI.T701]

DUFF, PATRICK, in Belfast, a letter of attorney, 1698. [PRONI.D1449.1.23A]

THE PEOPLE OF BELFAST, 1600-1799

DUGGAN, JAMES, a butcher, was admitted as a Freeman of Belfast in 1727. [TBB]

DUMVILL, WILLIAM, in Belfast, born 1740, died 1793. [Shankill MI, Belfast]

DUNBAR, JOHN, an attorney in Belfast, was admitted as a Freeman of Belfast in 1767. [TBB]

DUNCAN, DAVID, master of the Salmon of Belfast 1695. [NRS.E72.19.23]

DUNCAN, GEORGE, was admitted as a Freeman of Belfast in 1641, [TBB]; in Belfast, 1669. [PRONI.T307A]

DUNCAN, GEORGE, in Belfast, was apprenticed for five years aboard the Martha of Belfast in 1726. [PRONI.D354.390]

DUNLOP, HUGH, in Belfast, a deed, 1776. [PRONI.D199.8]; a lease in Church Lane, Belfast, 1789. [PRONI.D199.14]; a lease in Union Street, Belfast, in 1796. [PRONI.D438.4]

DUNLAP, JAMES, from Hollywood, was admitted as a Freeman of Belfast in 1728. [TBB]

DUNLAP, JANE, born 1763, died 1815. [New Burying Ground MI]

DUNLOP, JOHN, a butcher in Belfast, was admitted as a Freeman of Belfast in 1760. [TBB]

DUNN, DAVID, in Belfast, assignation of a tenement in Donegal Street, Belfast, 1781. [PRONI.D199.11/17]

DUNN, JAMES, born 1712, died 1804. [New Burying Ground MI]

DUNNING, ROBERT, a butcher in Belfast in 1622. [TBB]

THE PEOPLE OF BELFAST, 1600-1799

DUNNING, THOMAS, a butcher in Belfast in 1622. [TBB]

DUNWOODY, JOHN, in Belfast, 1669. [PRONI.T307A]

DYAT, HUGH, master of the Hanover of Belfast bound for Rotterdam and Malaga, 1738. [PRONI.354.576]

DYATT, JOHN, in Belfast, a lease in the High Street there in 1754. [PRONI.D509.62]

DYSON, RALPH, a butcher in Belfast in 1622. [TBB]

EALES, HUGH, a merchant in Belfast, 1668. [ActsPCCol.755/1041]

EASLAKE, WILLIAM, a joiner, was admitted as a Freeman of Belfast in 1725. [TBB]

EASSON, ..., master of the Prince of Wales of Belfast trading with Charleston, South Carolina, in 1763, 1767. [SCGaz.1540][TNA.CO5.511]

ECCLES, DAVID, a tailor and a rioter in Belfast, 1614. [OB.38]

ECCLES, GILBERT, a merchant, was admitted as a Free Commoner of Belfast in 1647. [TBB]

ECCLES, HUGH, a merchant in Belfast, was admitted as a Freeman of Belfast in 1656, and a burgess there in 1667, [TBB]; in Belfast 1669, [PRONI.T307A]; 1670, [TBB.116]; a bond, 1678, [Kirkcudbright Sheriff Court Deeds.266]; a burgess 1667 -1681. [BMF]

ECCLES, JAMES, a merchant in Belfast, a contract, 1690. [NRS.GD305.1.147.33]

ECCLES, JOHN, a merchant in Belfast, bound for France aboard the Content of Belfast in 1681. [SPDom.1681.228]

THE PEOPLE OF BELFAST, 1600-1799

ECHLIN, JAMES, MA, vicar of Belfast Corporation Church in 1695.

EDGAR, JOHN, a smith, was admitted as a Freeman of Belfast in 1725. [TBB]

EDWARD, JAMES, master of the bark Elizabeth of Belfast 1690. [NRS.E72.12.16]

EDWARD, JOHN, master of the bark Providence of Belfast 1683. [NRS.E72.12.7]

EDWARD, THOMAS, master of the bark Elizabeth of Belfast 1690. [NRS.E72.12.17]

EGGER, JAMES, master of the Prince of Wales of Belfast 1764. [TNA.CO5.511]

EGGER, JOSEPH, a lease in the High Street of Belfast in 1770. [PRONI.D199.4]

EGLISHAME, WILLIAM, master of the Margaret of Belfast 1682. [NRS.E72.1.5; E72.12.6]

ELDER, SAMUEL, born 1774, died 1838, husband of Martha …., born 1766, died 1817. [Shankill MI, Belfast]

ELLIOT, JOHN, sr., a merchant in Belfast, husband of Jane ……, born 1740, died 1802, parents of John Elliot jr., born 1780, died 1802. [New Burying Ground MI]

ELLIS, HENRY, a burgess, 1707. [BMF]

ELLIOT, JOHN, was admitted as a Freeman of Belfast in 1730. [TBB]

ELLIOT, ROBERT, born 1762, a merchant in Belfast, died 1837, husband of Anne ……, born 1780, died 1839. [New Burying Ground MI]

THE PEOPLE OF BELFAST, 1600-1799

EMERSON, WILLIAM, in Belfast, lease of a store in Legg's Lane, Belfast, 1792. [PRONI.D298.81]

ENGLISH, WILLIAM, a carpenter, was admitted as a Freeman of Belfast in 1726. [TBB]

ERVIN, JAMES, a coat measurer in Belfast, was admitted as a Freeman of Belfast in 1774. [TBB]

ESPLIN, JOHN, son of Michael Esplin a sailor in Belfast, apprentice of James Esplin a tanner in Edinburgh, 1737. [REA]

ESSON, ..., master of the <u>Prince of Wales of Belfast</u> trading with South Carolina, 1764/1767. [TNA.CO5.511]

ESSPY, HUGH, a merchant in Belfast, a deed, 1676. [NRS.RD4.39.120]; a merchant from Belfast, a merchant in Kirkwall, Orkney, in 1679. [NRS.AC7.75]

EVANS, JOHN, of the parish of Carmoney, was admitted as a Freeman of Belfast in 1746. [TBB]

EWART, GEORGE, a merchant from Londonderry, was admitted as a Freeman of Belfast in 1728. [TBB]

EWART, WILLIAM, born 1758, died 1851, husband of Sarah ....., born 1861, died 1833. [New Burying Ground MI]

EWING, JOHN, a merchant in Belfast, was admitted as a Freeman of Belfast in 1774. [TBB]; a banker in Belfast, 1787. [TBB]

FARQUHAR, HENRY, in Belfast, 1669. [PRONI.T307A]

FARQUHAR, JOHN, was admitted as a Freeman of Belfast in 1726. [TBB]

FEE, DAVID, in Belfast, a lease, 1770. [PRONI.D509.458]

THE PEOPLE OF BELFAST, 1600-1799

FEE, SAMUEL, born 1735, died 1802. [Shankill MI, Belfast]

FELL, ..., of Pilafowder, was admitted as a Freeman of Belfast in 1753. [TBB]

FERES, ELIZABETH, born 1760, died 1794.[Shankill MI, Belfast]

FERGUSON, FRANCIS, of the Falls, was admitted as a Freeman of Belfast in 1771. [TBB]

FERGUSON, GEORGE, a merchant in Belfast, was admitted as a Freeman of Belfast in 1760. [TBB]; in Belfast, a lease in 1770. [PRONI.D509.460]

FERGUSON, JAMES, a linen merchant in Belfast, an account book, 1771-1783. [PRONI.D468.1]

FERGUSON, JAMES, a merchant in Belfast, 1789. [PRONI.D275.14]; in Linenhall Street, Belfast, a lease of Lower Malone, Belfast, in 1796. [PRONI.D298.89]

FERGUSON, JOHN, owner of the Sara of Belfast, was admitted as a Freeman of Belfast in 1655. [TBB]

FERGUSON, JOHN, a cooper, was admitted as a Freeman of Belfast in 1725. [TBB]

FERGUSON, JOHN, a merchant in Belfast, was admitted as a Freeman of Belfast in 1760. [TBB]

FERGUSON, JOHN, a farmer, was admitted as a Freeman of Belfast in 1783. [TBB]

FERGUSON, SAMUEL, a farmer, was admitted as a Freeman of Belfast in 1778. [TBB]

FERGUSON, WILLIAM, a publican in Belfast, was admitted as a Freeman of Belfast in 1772. [TBB]

THE PEOPLE OF BELFAST, 1600-1799

FERGUSON, WITNEY J., born 1778, a tailor from Belfast, was naturalised in South Carolina in 1799. [NARA.M1183]

FERRA, MATTHEW, the parish clerk, was admitted as a Free Commoner of Belfast in 1654. [TBB]

FERRIER, WILLIAM, master of the Martin of Belfast 1689. [NRS.E72.19.15]

FIFE, Mrs MARY, born 1695, wife of Thomas Fife a carpenter in Belfast, died 1772. [Shankill MI, Belfast]

FIFE, THOMAS, a carpenter, was admitted as a Freeman of Belfast in 1728. [TBB]

FINLAY, JOHN, in Belfast, 1669. [PRONI.T307A]

FINLAY, RICHARD, town sergeant of Belfast, 1738. [PRONI.D354.1011]

FISHER, JOHN, master and merchant of the Mary of Belfast 1683. [NRS.E2.12.8]

FISHER, JOHN, a porter, was admitted as a Freeman of Belfast in 1737. [TBB]

FISHER, JOHN, a saddler, was admitted as a Freeman of Belfast in 1739. [TBB]

FITZSIMMONS, SAMUEL, a lease of Graham's Entry, Belfast, in 1792. [PRONI.D298.79]

FIVEY, JAMES, a merchant, was admitted as a Freeman of Belfast in 1733. [TBB]

FIVEY, JOHN, a merchant, was admitted as a Freeman of Belfast in 1737. [TBB]

FLEMING, FRANCIS, a laborer, was admitted as a Freeman of Belfast in 1658. [TBB]

THE PEOPLE OF BELFAST, 1600-1799

FLEMMING, JOHN, former apprentice to James Magee a carpenter, was admitted as a Freeman of Belfast in 1728. [TBB]

FLEMING, THOMAS, master of the Carolina of Belfast 1734. [TNA.CO5.508]

FLEMING, SAMUEL, in Hollywood, was admitted as a Freeman of Belfast in 1728. [TBB]

FLETCHER, ELIZABETH, in Belfast, a lease, 1691. [PRONI.D412.2]

FLETCHER, PAUL, an adventurer who was granted land in the south-east quarter of the barony of Belfast, 1643. [SPI.1642-1659: 354]

FOGG, ELLYS, a merchant, was admitted as a Free Stapler of Belfast in 1637. [TBB]

FOLLIOT, JOHN, in Belfast, a letter, 1690. [PRONI.D429.18]

FORBES, JOHN, a husbandman in Belfast, was admitted as a Free Commoner of Belfast in 1645, [TBB]; in Belfast, 1669. [PRONI.T307A]

FORBES, WILLIAM, a wheelwright, was admitted as a Freeman of Belfast in 1730. [TBB]

FOREMAN, JAMES, in Belfast, lease of the Cornmarket, Belfast, 1727. [PRONI.D509.48]

FORREST, GEORGE, a seaman from Belfast, to be released from Edinburgh or Canongate tollbooth, 1689. [RPCS.XIII.554]; master of the William and Robert of Belfast 1689. [NRS.E72.19.14]

FORSYTH, EDWARD, in the Falls, was admitted as a Freeman of Belfast in 1730. [TBB]

THE PEOPLE OF BELFAST, 1600-1799

FORSYTH, JAMES, a physician in Belfast, a trustee, a bond, 1808. [NRS.GD60.163]

FORSYTH, JOHN, a smith, was admitted as a Freeman of Belfast in 1726. [TBB]

FORSYTH, ROBERT, in the Falls, was admitted as a Freeman of Belfast in 1730. [TBB]

FORSYTH, WILLIAM, in the Liberties of Belfast, 1669. [PRONI.T307A]

FORTESCUE, HENRY, postmaster of Belfast, was admitted as a Freeman of Belfast in 1767. [TBB]

FOSTER, RICHARD, was admitted as a Freeman of Belfast in 1640. [TBB]

FOSTER, ROBERT, a gentleman, was admitted as a burgess of Belfast in 1642. [TBB]; Sovereign there in 1635. [TBB]

FRAME, Mrs, a widow in Belfast, 1669. [PRONI.T307A]

FRISSALL, ALEXANDER, a carman, was admitted as a Freeman of Belfast in 1728. [TBB]

FRISSELL, GEORGE, a mealman, was admitted as a Free Commoner of Belfast in 1654. [TBB]

FRIZZELL, DANIEL, in Belfast, 1669. [PRONI.T307A]

FRIZZELL, JOHN, in Belfast, 1669. [PRONI.T307A]

FULLERTON, ROBERT, in Belfast, 1669. [PRONI.T307A]

FULTON, JOHN, in Carmony, was admitted as a Freeman of Belfast in 1783. [TBB]

FULTON, THOMAS, in Belfast, 1669. [PRONI.T307A]

FULTON, WILLIAM, in Belfast, 1669. [PRONI.T307A]

THE PEOPLE OF BELFAST, 1600-1799

FULTON, WILLIAM, born 1697 near Belfast, son of Thomas Fulton, a student at Trinity College, Dublin, in 1703, graduated B.A. in 1708, and M.A. in 1711. [AD]

FULTON, ..., in the barony of Belfast, 1659. [C]

GABBY, JOHN, a tailor, was admitted as a Freeman of Belfast in 1731. [TBB]

GALLERY, JAMES, a carpenter, was admitted as a Freeman of Belfast in 1725. [TBB]

GALLOP, THOMAS, a smith, was admitted as a Free Commoner of Belfast in 1650. [TBB]

GALPHIN, JOHN, a burgess of Belfast in 1646. [TBB]

GALT, JOHN, a husbandman, was admitted as a Free Commoner of Belfast in 1649. [TBB]

GALT, JOHN, master of the Friendship of Belfast trading with Charleston, South Carolina, in 1718. [TNA.CO5.510]

GALT, JOHN, a smith and a merchant in Belfast, was admitted as a Freeman of Belfast in 1760. [TBB]

GAMBLE, ROBERT, born 1776, died 1836, father of John, born 1809, died 1828 in New Orleans, and of Hamilton, born 1820, died 1839 in New Orleans. [Clifton Street MI, Belfast]

GARNER, NICHOLAS, was admitted as a Freeman of Belfast in 1643. [TBB]; in Belfast, 1645. [TBB]

GARNER, RICHARD, master of the Isabel of Belfast trading with Barbados, 1682. [NRS.E72.19.5]

GARRET, PATRICK, a tailor, was admitted as a Freeman of Belfast in 1752. [TBB]

THE PEOPLE OF BELFAST, 1600-1799

GARRETT, THOMAS, born 1774, solicitor in Belfast, died 1837, husband of Anne Neilson, born 1782, died 1857. [New Burying Ground MI]

GARVEN, THOMAS, master of the Janet of Belfast captured by a Parliamentarian vessel when bound from Bordeaux to Carrickfergus in 1644, [TNA.HCA.Exams.13.50.204]; a merchant of Ayr, was admitted as a Free Stapler of Belfast in 1645. [TBB]

GASKIN, ROBERT, an ale-seller, was admitted as a Freeman of Belfast in 1728. [TBB]

GATELY, RICHARD, a gentleman, was admitted as a burgess of Belfast in 1643. [TBB]

GAUSLEY, JOHN, a clothier, was admitted as a Freeman of Belfast in 1639. [TBB]

GEAR, ARTHUR, a gentleman, was admitted as a Freeman of Belfast in 1728. [TBB]

GELSTON, THOMAS, a soap-boiler, was admitted as a Freeman of Belfast in 1726. [TBB]

GELSTON, THOMAS, a surgeon in Belfast, died 1801, husband of Agnes Gunning, died 1810. [New Burying Ground MI]

GEMBELL, JAMES, merchant aboard the Robert and John of Belfast in 1689. [NRS.E72.20.14]

GEMMELL, JAMES, a merchant in Belfast, a deed, 1687. [NRS.RD3.66.666]

GEMMILL, ROBERT, born 1744, a merchant in Belfast, died there in 1808. [SM.70.479]

GETTY, JAMES, a merchant in Belfast, was admitted as a Freeman of Belfast in 1761. [TBB]; a lease in Goose Lane, Belfast, 1779. [PRONI.D298.40]

THE PEOPLE OF BELFAST, 1600-1799

GIBBS, THOMAS, born 1775, died 1836, husband of Sarah ....., born 1790, died 1840. [New Burying Ground MI]

GIBB, WILLIAM, a merchant in Belfast, 1690. [NRS.E72.3.20]

GIBSON, ARCHIBALD, in Belfast, a letter, 1754. [PRONI.D364.752]

GIBSON, HENRY, of the Falls, was admitted as a Freeman of Belfast in 1771. [TBB]

GIBSON, HUGH, a glazier, was admitted as a Freeman of Belfast in 1728. [TBB]

GIBSON, JAMES, born 1747, died 1812, husband of Sarah...[Shankill MI, Belfast]

GIBSON, JOHN, born 1651 in Belfast, son of George Gibson, a student at Trinity College, Dublin, in 1673. [AD]

GIBSON, JOHN, a merchant from Glasgow, in Belfast, 1685. [NRS.JC39.87]

GIBSON, JOHN, a tailor, was admitted as a Freeman of Belfast in 1752. [TBB]

GIBSON, JOHN, born 1769, died 1827, husband of Sarah .... born 1762, died 1827. [New Burying Ground MI]

GIBSON, PATRICK, a baker, was admitted as a Freeman of Belfast in 1725. [TBB]

GIBSON, ROBERT, was admitted as a Freeman of Belfast in 1637. [TBB]

GIBSON, ROBERT, a tailor, was admitted as a Freeman of Belfast in 1752. [TBB]

THE PEOPLE OF BELFAST, 1600-1799

GILBERT, CLAUDIUS, vicar of Belfast Corporation Church in 1668.

GILCHRIST, JOHN, merchant on the St Andrew of Belfast 1691. [NRS.E72.19.21] GILL, THOMAS, a burgess of Belfast, 1639, 1645. [TBB]; who was previously disenfranchised, was readmitted as a Free Commoner of Belfast in 1647. [TBB]

GILLESPIE, DAVID, in Belfast, born 1768, died 1828, [Shankill MI, Belfast]

GILLETT, CHRISTOPHER, was admitted as a Freeman of Belfast in 1644. [TBB]

GILLETT, JOHN, a tanner in Belfast, son of Freeman, was admitted as a Free Commoner of Belfast in 1645. [TBB]

GILLIS, JOHN, of Ballymacarrit, was admitted as a Freeman of Belfast in 1773. [TBB]

GILLIS, THOMAS, of Killead, born 1739, died 1816, husband of Agnes …., born 1749, died 1822, parents of James, born 1785, died 1796, William, born 1785, died 1823, Joseph, born 1787, died 1846, and Benjamin, born 1790, died 1837. [Shankill MI, Belfast]

GILMORE, ALEXANDER, a shopkeeper, was admitted as a Freeman of Belfast in 1725. [TBB]

GILMOUR, JOHN, master of the Joan of Belfast, 1682. [NRS.E72.19.6]

GILPATRICK, THOMAS, was admitted as a Freeman of Belfast in 1639. [TBB]

GISBY, WILLIAM, master of the Robert Trader of Belfast 1770. [NRS.E504.15.18]

THE PEOPLE OF BELFAST, 1600-1799

GLASGOW, JAMES, in Belfast, 1669. [PRONI.T307A]; master of the James of Belfast from 1661 to 1675. [BMF]

GLEN, JOHN, a maltster, was admitted as a Freeman of Belfast in 1725. [TBB]

GLENHOLMES, JOHN, born 1748, died 1828. [Shankill MI, Belfast]

GLOVER, JAMES, merchant on the Three Williams of Belfast 1682. [NRS.E72.3.10]

GLOVER, JAMES, master of the Rose of Belfast 1689. [NRS.E72.12.15; E72.3.21]

GLOVER, JOHN, a baker, was admitted as a Freeman of Belfast in 1728. [TBB]

GODFREY, BARBARA, born 1769, daughter of the Rev. Dr Godfrey in Belfast married the Earl of Donegal, in London, 1790. [SM.52.516]

GODFREY, THOMAS, a tailor, was admitted as a Freeman of Belfast in 1639. [TBB]

GOFFIGAN, ARTHUR, a butcher in Belfast, was admitted as a Freeman of Belfast in 1760. [TBB]

GOLFIN, HUGH, a carpenter in Belfast, 1654. [TBB]

GOOD, JOHN, master of the Margaret of Belfast 1672. [NRS.E72.10.3]

GORDON, HUGH, Controller of the Port of Belfast, 1769. [PRONI.D303.2]

GORDON, JAMES, a merchant in Belfast, 1725. [NRS.AC9.1050/1071]

GORDON, JAMES, a tailor, was admitted as a Freeman of Belfast in 1728. [TBB]

THE PEOPLE OF BELFAST, 1600-1799

GORDON, JOHN, in Belfast, 1669. [PRONI.T307A]

GORDON, JOHN, a merchant in Belfast, 1728, 1734. [NRS.AC9.1050][PRONI.D354.494]

GORDON, ROBERT, was admitted as a Freeman of Belfast in 1733. [TBB]

GORDON, ROBERT, in Belfast, was admitted as a Freeman of Belfast in 1772. [TBB]

GORDON, WILLIAM, a merchant in Belfast, was admitted as a Freeman of Belfast in 1760. [TBB]

GOSE, MARTIN, was admitted as a Freeman of Belfast in 1647. [TBB]

GOSS, ROBERT, master of the <u>Marigold of Belfast</u> trading with Madeira, 1690. [NRS.E72.19.22]

GOUDY, GILBERT, in Belfast, a lease, 1770. [PRONI.D509.455]

GOUGH, PATRICK, was admitted as a Freeman of Belfast in 1643. [TBB]

GOYE, JOHN, a joiner, was admitted as a Freeman of Belfast in 1639. [TBB]

GRAHAM, FRANCIS, an innkeeper in Belfast, was admitted as a Freeman of Belfast in 1752. [TBB]; a lease of McMunn's Entry on the High Street of Belfast, 1767. [PRONI.D298.30]

GRAHAM, HUE, was admitted as a Freeman of Belfast in 1783. [TBB]

GRAHAM, JAMES, in Belfast, a lease in Linenhall Lane, Belfast, 1780. [PRONI.D509.613]

THE PEOPLE OF BELFAST, 1600-1799

GRAHAM, JOHN, a laborer, was admitted as a Freeman of Belfast in 1658. [TBB]

GRAHAM, JOHN, in Belfast, a lease in Green Street, Belfast, 1802. [PRONI.D199.25]

GRAHAM, ..., in the barony of Belfast, 1659. [C]

GRAINGER, ARTHUR, a lease in Skipper's Lane, Belfast, 1787. [PRONI.D238.60]

GRANGER, JAMES, a baker, was admitted as a Freeman of Belfast in 1731. [TBB]

GRAY, GAVIN, a huckster, was admitted as a Freeman of Belfast in 1725. [TBB]

GRAY, WILLIAM, junior, a merchant in Belfast, a deed, 1752. [NRS.RD4.178.2.305]

GREEN, JOHN, born 1742, died 1818, father of Robert Green in Montreal. [Shankill MI, Belfast]

GREEN, JOSEPH, in Belfast, 1754. [PRONI.D270.5]; a burgess of Belfast, a letter 1754. [PRONI.D354.1007]

GREGG, JOHN, master of the _Adventure of Belfast_ in 1661. [BMF]

GREGG, JOHN, a merchant, was admitted as a Freeman of Belfast in 1725. [TBB]

GREGG, JOHN, jr., a merchant in Belfast, a merchant in Belfast, was admitted as a Freeman of Belfast in 1758. [TBB]; a bond, 1790. [PRONI.D491.50]

GREGG, THOMAS, a member of the Third Presbyterian Meeting House, Belfast, 1749. [PRONI.D298.16]

GREGG, THOMAS, a merchant in Belfast, co-partner in Gregg, Cunningham and Company in New York, deed

THE PEOPLE OF BELFAST, 1600-1799

of copartnery, 1761, [PRONI.D270.6];an emigration agent, [BNL:29.4.1763]; a lease in 1774, [PRONI.D409.1]; a conveyance of premises in Skipper's Lane, Belfast, 1781. [PRONI.D238.56]; a co-partner of the Belfast Glass House Company, deed of partnership, 1791. [PRONI.]

GREGG, WILLIAM, a merchant in Belfast in 1755. [PRONI.D491.15]

GREGG, WILLIAM, jr., a merchant in Belfast, was admitted as a Freeman of Belfast in 1758. [TBB]

GREGORY, THOMAS, in Belfast, a lease, 1732. [PRONI.D199.1]

GREIG, ANDREW, master of the snow …….of Belfast trading with Virginia, 1689. [RPCS.13.538]

GREIG, WILLIAM, a merchant in Belfast, was admitted as a burgess of St Andrews, Fife, in 1735. [StABR]

GRIFFIN, JOHN, in Belfast, a lease of Goose Lane in Belfast, 1670. [PRONI.D509.21]

GRIFFITH, JAMES, born 1713, died 1797. [Shankill MI, Belfast]

GRIFFITH, THOMAS, son of James Griffith above, born 1759, died 1838. [Shankill MI, Belfast]

GRIFFITH, WILLIAM, was admitted as a Freeman of Belfast in 1640. [TBB]

GROME, or SLYE, THOMAS, in Belfast, 1651. [TBB]

GURNER, JAMES, a burgess 1707. [BMF]

GUTHRIE, JAMES, master of the Prosperity of Belfast 1691. [NRS.E72.19.21]

THE PEOPLE OF BELFAST, 1600-1799

HACKETT, JOHN, a blacksmith, was admitted as a Freeman of Belfast in 1731. [TBB]

HADDEN, JOHN, in Belfast in 1645. [TBB]

HADDOCK, JOHN, master of the Nightingale of Belfast, 1627. [CDG.2.587][ERG.II.586]; a burgess of Belfast in 1640. [TBB]

HADDOCK, ROGER, in Belfast, and Eleanor Crawford in Belfast, a marriage settlement, 1709. [PRONI.D671.D8.3.2] a burgess 1708. [BMF]

HALL, JOSEPH, a bell-founder, was admitted as a Freeman of Belfast in 1726. [TBB]

HALLIDAY, Dr ALEXANDER HENRY, in Belfast, a lease in 1770. [PRONI.D509.469]; a letter re his brother in Charleston, South Carolina, 1782. [RIA:Charlemont ms.d/h/i/l]

HALLIDAY, HENRY, born 1747, a physician, died in Belfast 1802. [SM.64.448]

HALTRIDGE, JOHN, a burgess, 1707. [BMF]

HAMIL, HANS, master of the Friendship of Belfast trading with Virginia, 1699. [TNA.CO5.1441]

HAMIL, JAMES, a merchant, was admitted as a Freeman of Belfast in 1777. [TBB]

HAMILTON, ARCHIBALD, a merchant in Belfast, was admitted as a burgess and guilds-brother of Ayr, 1719. [ABR]

HAMILTON, ARCHIBALD, from Ballymechan, was admitted as a Freeman of Belfast in 1728. [TBB]

HAMILTON, ARTHUR, a merchant in Belfast, trading with Cadiz, Spain, 1712. [PRONI.D354.359]

THE PEOPLE OF BELFAST, 1600-1799

HAMILTON, CHARLES, a cooper, was admitted as a Freeman of Belfast in 1725. [TBB]

HAMILTON, FRANCIS, a merchant, was admitted as a Freeman of Belfast in 1731. [TBB]

HAMILTON, HANS, was admitted as a burgess of Belfast in 1711. [TBB]

HAMILTON, HANS, a shoemaker in County Tyrone, was admitted as a Freeman of Belfast in 1730. [TBB]

HAMILTON, HENRY, a chapman, was admitted as a Freeman of Belfast in 1728. [TBB]

HAMILTON, HUGH, a merchant aboard the Betty of Belfast 1681. [NRS.E72.3.9]

HAMILTON, JAMES, a merchant in Belfast, was admitted as a burgess and guilds-brother of Glasgow in 1707. [GBR]

HAMILTON, JAMES, co-owner of the Priscilla of Belfast bound for Bremen, Germany, 1720. [PRONI.D354.373]

HAMILTON, JAMES, a gentleman, was admitted as a Freeman of Belfast in 1728. [TBB]

HAMILTON, JAMES, a gentleman, was admitted as a Freeman of Belfast in 1733. [TBB]

HAMILTON, JOHN, was admitted as a burgess of Belfast in 1678. [TBB]; a merchant in Belfast, a deed, 1682. [NRS.RD2.58.21]; a burgess 1678-1687. [BMF]

HAMILTON, JOHN, a merchant in Belfast, was admitted as a burgess and guilds-brother of Ayr, 1697. [ABR]

HAMILTON, JOHN, a banker in Belfast, 1789. [PRONI.D270.15][TBB]

THE PEOPLE OF BELFAST, 1600-1799

HAMILTON, PATRICK, a gentleman and councillor of Belfast in 1678. [TBB]

HAMILTON, WILLIAM, a seaman from Belfast, was killed at the taking of Carrickfergus, husband of Barbara McDonald, father of three children, before 1690. [RPCS.XV.227]

HAMILTON, WILLIAM, a cooper, was admitted as a Freeman of Belfast in 1725. [TBB]

HANNAH, ANDREW, a publican in Belfast, was admitted as a Freeman of Belfast in 1773. [TBB]

HANNAH, JAMES, born 1765, died 1837, husband of Elizabeth ...., born 1767, died 1840. [Shankill MI, Belfast]

HANNA, HUGH, in the Liberties of Belfast, 1669. [PRONI.T307A]

HANNA, JOHN, a merchant in Belfast aboard the Content of Belfast trading with France in 1681, [SPDom.1681.228]; merchant on the James of Belfast 1686. [NRS.E72.12.12]

HANNA, PATRICK, in the Liberties of Belfast, 1669. [PRONI.T307A]

HANNA, THOMAS, a tailor and Freeman of Belfast in 1673. [TBB]

HANNAH, WILLIAM, born 1794, a mariner from Belfast, was naturalised in South Carolina in 1828. [NARA.M1183]

HANNINGTON, THOMAS, a burgess of Belfast in 1639. [TBB]

HARDEN, JOHN, a smith in Belfast in 1647. [TBB]

THE PEOPLE OF BELFAST, 1600-1799

HARDIN, THOMAS, was admitted as a Freeman of Belfast in 1777. [TBB]

HARDY, THOMAS, a burgess of Belfast, 1645. [TBB]

HARDY, WILLIAM, a farmer in the Falls, was admitted as a Freeman of Belfast in 1737. [TBB]

HARMAN, CORNELIUS, a burgess of Belfast in 1632. [TBB]

HARPER, PETER, a merchant in Belfast, testament, 1729, Comm. Edinburgh. [NRS]

HARRINGTON, THOMAS, in Belfast, 1643. [TBB]

HARRIS, SAMUEL, a gentleman, was admitted as a Free Commoner of Belfast in 1652. [TBB]

HARRIS, WILLIAM, in Belfast, a lease in West Street, Belfast, 1790. [PRONI.D491.41]

HARRISON, EDWARD, a burgess 1680-1700. [BMF]

HARRISON, HUGH, born 1771, a mariner from Belfast, was naturalised in South Carolina in 1804. [NARA.M1183]

HARRISON, JOHN, master and merchant of the <u>Joan of Belfast</u> trading with Madeira, 1691. [NRS.E72.19.22]

HARRISON, JOHN, son of John Harrison of Newtown, was admitted as a Freeman of Belfast in 1748. [TBB]

HARRISON, MATTHEW, a gentleman in Belfast, 1659. [C]

HARRISON, MICHAEL, in Magrilean, barony of Belfast, 1659. [C]

HARRISON, MICHAEL, a gentleman burgess of Belfast, 1705-1709. [BMF]

THE PEOPLE OF BELFAST, 1600-1799

HARRISON, ROBERT, an attorney, was admitted as a Freeman of Belfast in 1752. [TBB]

HARRISON, WILLIAM, son of John Harrison in Newtown, a merchant, was admitted as a Freeman of Belfast in 1748. [TBB]

HART, HENRY, a merchant from Londonderry, was admitted as a Freeman of Belfast in 1729. [TBB]

HASELDEN, ROGER, in Belfast in 1645. [TBB]

HASLIP, THOMAS, a weaver, was admitted as a Free Commoner of Belfast in 1647. [TBB]

HASTIE, JOHN, master of the Mary of Belfast in 1685. [NRS.E72.12.11]

HATHORN, HUGH, master of the Jupiter of Belfast 1765. [NRS.E504.4.4]

HATHORN, ROBERT, a miller in Belfast, was admitted as a Freeman of Belfast in 1774. [TBB]

HAVEN, STEPHEN, master of the Hopewell of Belfast trading with Barbados and Charleston, South Carolina, in 1733-1734. [TNA.CO5.509]

HAVEN, STEPHEN, jr, son of the Sovereign Stephen Haven, in Belfast, was admitted as a Freeman of Belfast in 1760. [TBB]

HAVEN, WILLIAM, a merchant in Belfast, son of Steven Haven the Sovereign, was admitted as a Freeman of Belfast in 1760. [TBB]

HAWKINS, HUGH, a merchant in Belfast, a lease, 1687. [PRONI.D671.D1.3.8]

THE PEOPLE OF BELFAST, 1600-1799

HAY, JOHN, a bookseller in Belfast, son of Hugh Hay a merchant in Ayr and his wife Janet Jamieson, 1746. [NRS.S/H]

HAZLETT, or GAW, JANE, wife of Henry Hazlett, an heir of Patrick Gaw in Belfast, 1792. [PRONI.D298.80]

HEATHCOTT, BENJAMIN, an adventurer who was granted land in the south-west-quarter of the barony of Belfast, 1643. [SPI.1642-1659: 354]

HEATHCOTT, JOSEPH, an adventurer who was granted land in the south-west-quarter of the barony of Belfast, 1643. [SPI.1642-1659: 354]

HENDERSON, BENJAMIN, born 1731, died 1803, husband of Catherine ……., born 1736, died 1808, parents of Benjamin Henderson of Legoneil, born 1771, died 1823. [Shankill MI, Belfast]

HENDERSON, DAVID, son of Margaret Henderson, was apprenticed for six years aboard the Prince George of Belfast in 1718, a bond, 1718. [PRONI.D354.366/367]

HENDERSON, DAVID, a stationer in Belfast, witness to the will of John Buchanan, probate, 1784, Dublin.

HENDERSON, DAVID, a merchant in Belfast, was admitted as a Freeman of Belfast in 1760. [TBB]; in Belfast, lease in Church Lane, Belfast, 1770. [PRONI.D509.471]

HENDERSON, HUGH, in Belfast, a lease re Fore Plantation, Belfast, 1789. [PRONI.D199.16]

HENDERSON, JOHN, a merchant aboard the Margaret of Belfast 1682. [NRS.E72.12.5]

HENDERSON, JOHN, born 1747, died 1832, husband of Rebecca ……, born 1757, died 1813. [Shankill MI, Belfast]

THE PEOPLE OF BELFAST, 1600-1799

HENDERSON, JOHN, a merchant in Belfast, was admitted as a Freeman of Belfast in 1774. [TBB]; a lease of Rosemary Lane, Belfast, 1787. [PRONI.CR3.32.B1.7]

HENDERSON, ROBERT, in Belfast in 1645. [TBB]

HENDERSON, ROBERT, a watchmaker, was admitted as a Freeman of Belfast in 1728. [TBB]

HENDERSON, WILLIAM, a weaver, was admitted as a Freeman of Belfast, 1650. [TBB]; in Belfast, 1669. [PRONI.T307A]

HENRY, JAMES, of Skegenearl, was admitted as a Freeman of Belfast in 1747. [TBB]

HEPBURN, DAVID, master of the William and Joan of Belfast bound for Virginia, a charter party, 1679. [NRS.RD3.48.513]; in Belfast, a deed, 1680. [NRS.RD4.47.866]; master of the St Lucar of Belfast bound for New York in 1680. [SPAWI.1680.1602]

HEPBURN, PATRICK, a Lieutenant of Maxwell's Regiment, was admitted as Free Commoner of Belfast in 1647. [TBB]

HERBERTSON, ALEXANDER, a wright and looking-glass maker in Glasgow, eloped with Jean Brodie, a servant, to Belfast in 1726. [NRS.CC8.5.3]

HERD, RICHARD, master of the Betty of Belfast in 1746. [NRS.E504.4.1]

HERRIES, JOHN, a merchant aboard the Joan of Belfast trading with Madeira, 1691. [NRS.E72.19.22]

HERRON, JOHN, a shoemaker, was admitted as a Freeman of Belfast in 1726. [TBB]

THE PEOPLE OF BELFAST, 1600-1799

HERRON, WILLIAM, was admitted as a Freeman of Belfast in 1728. [TBB]

HEYLAND, HERCULES, in Belfast, a lease of Old Park in Belfast, 1770.[PRONI.D509.474]; lease re Donegal Street, Belfast, 1781. [PRONI.D195.11]

HEYLAND, ROWLEY, in Belfast, and Mary MacDonnell in Dublin, a marriage settlement in 1780. [PRONI.D300.1.6.6.6]

HILL, MOYSES, a lease in Belfast, 1606. [TBB]

HILL, SAMUEL, born 1718, died 1753. [Shankill MI, Belfast]

HILLARY, JOSHUA, in Belfast, lease in Brown Street, Belfast, in 1796. [PRONI.D438.3]

HISLOP, THOMAS, in Belfast, 1669. [PRONI.T307A]

HOBSON, HUGH, of Bowes Hill, born 1775, died 1852, husband of Margaret ……., born 1778, died 1860. [Shankill MI, Belfast]

HODGES, JOHN, a gentleman, was admitted as a Free Stapler of Belfast in 1638. [TBB]

HODGKINS, THOMAS, was admitted as a Free Stapler of Belfast in 1635. [TBB]

HODGKINSON, RICHARD, a gentleman in Mill Street, Belfast, husband of Sarah Hodgkinson, father of Richard and Jean, probate 1720, Dublin.

HOLMES, EDWARD, in Belfast, 1632. [TBB]

HOLMES, GABRIEL, master of the <u>Gabriel of Belfast</u> in 1682. [NRS.E72.19.5]

THE PEOPLE OF BELFAST, 1600-1799

HOLMES, JAMES, master of the Joan of Belfast in 1691. [NRS.E72.19.21]

HOLMES, JOHN, master of the John of Belfast in 1667. [NRS.E72.3.2]

HOLMES, JOHN, a merchant in Belfast, a lease in Upper Malone, Belfast, in 1770, [PRONI.D509.477]; a will, 1777. [PRONI.D12555.3.32A][NAI.T703]; a lease in 1770, [PRONI.D332.1]; a lease of Rosemary Lane, Belfast, 1787. [PRONI.CR3.32.B1.7]; a banker in Belfast, 1787. [TBB]; a lease in 1792. [PRONI.D332.3]; a merchant in Belfast, later in Dublin, probate 1779. [NAI.T703]

HOOD, HUGH, master of the Arthur and Ann of Belfast trading with Charleston, South Carolina, in 1719. [TNA.CO5.508]

HORSMAN, ANTHONY, a gentleman in Ballymey in the barony of Belfast in 1659. [C]

HOSKINS, RICHARD, a blacksmith, was admitted as a Freeman of Belfast in 1730. [TBB]

HOUGHTON, ARTHUR, a butcher, was admitted as a Free Commoner of Belfast in 1652, [TBB]

HOUSTON, JAMES, a carman, was admitted as a Freeman of Belfast in 1728. [TBB]

HOUSTON, WILLIAM, a merchant in Belfast, was admitted as a burgess and guilds-brother of Glasgow in 1715. [GBR]

HOY, PATRICK, a baker, was admitted as a Freeman of Belfast in 1746. [TBB]

HUDDLESTON, JOHN, a tailor, was admitted as a Freeman of Belfast in 1650. [TBB]; in Belfast, 1669. [PRONI.T307A]

THE PEOPLE OF BELFAST, 1600-1799

HUDSON, CHRISTOPHER, a tanner in Belfast, was admitted as a Freeman there in 1776. [TBB]

HUDSON, JOHN, a burgess of Belfast in 1639. [TBB]

HUGGIN, ROBERT, master of the Beattie of Belfast 1681. [NRS.E72.20.6]

HUGHS, JAMES, a farmer, was admitted as a Freeman of Belfast in 1726. [TBB]

HUGHS, JOHN, farmer of Carmony, was admitted as a Freeman of Belfast in 1726. [TBB]

HUGHS, JOSEPH, a merchant, was admitted as a Freeman of Belfast in 1726. [TBB]

HUGHSON, JOHN, in Belfast in 1645. [TBB]

HUGHSTON, RALPH, was admitted as a Free Commoner of Belfast in 1645. [TBB]

HUNTER, GEORGE, a wig-maker, was admitted as a Freeman of Belfast in 1726. [TBB]

HUNTER, HENRY, a grocer in Belfast was admitted as a Freeman there in 1781. [TBB]

HUNTER, JOHN, in the Liberties of Belfast, 1669. [PRONI.T307A]

HUNTER, MARY, in Belfast, a deed, 1799. [PRONI.D302.2.1.100.36]

HUNTER, MATTHEW, in Belfast, a deed, 1799. [PRONI.D302.2.1.100.36]

HUNTER, ROBERT, in Belfast, 1669. [PRONI.T307A]; a tailor and Freeman of Belfast in 1673, [TBB]; a merchant aboard the Charlemont of Belfast in 1678. [NRS.E72.3.4]

THE PEOPLE OF BELFAST, 1600-1799

HUNTER, …….., master of the Loyal Charles of Belfast 1699. [TBB]

HURD, JOHN, servant to Mr Collier, was admitted as a Freeman of Belfast in 1730. [TBB]

HUTCHISON, ANDREW, owner of the William of Belfast 1683. [NRS.E72.12.7]; a merchant in Belfast, a deed, 1688. [NRS.RD3.69.484]

HUTCHINSON, HANS, a farmer, was admitted as a Freeman of Belfast in 1728. [TBB]

HUTCHISON, WILLIAM, a shopkeeper was admitted as a Freeman of Belfast in 1731. [TBB]

HYDE, Mrs MARGARET, in Belfast, a deed, 1800. [PRONI.D270.20]

HYDE, SAMUEL, a merchant in Belfast, trading with Spain and Gibraltar, 1734. [PRONI.D354.493]

HYDE, SAMUEL, a merchant in Belfast, was admitted as a Freeman of Belfast in 1762, [TBB]; 1789. [PRONI.D270.13]

HYLAND, ROWLEY, in Longford Lodge, was admitted as a Freeman of Belfast in 1774. [TBB]

HYNDMAN, ANDREW, in Belfast, executor of Mary McWalters in Belfast, 1781. [PRONI.D199.10]

HYNDMAN, ARCHIBALD, in Belfast, a lease in North Street, Belfast, 1751. [PRONI.D298.18]

HYNDMAN, HUGH, in Belfast, a deed, 1726. [PRONI.D298.59]

HYNDMAN, HUGH, a lease of Rosemary Lane, Belfast, 1787. [PRONI.CR3.32.B1.7]; a co-partner of the Belfast

THE PEOPLE OF BELFAST, 1600-1799

Glass House Company, deed of partnership, 1791. [PRONI.]; in Belfast, 1792. [PRONI.D298.80]

HYNDMAN, MARGARET, in Belfast, a lease, 1778. [PRONI.D298.44]

HYNDMAN, ROBERT, in Belfast, a deed, 1726. [PRONI.D298.59]

HYNDMAN, ROBERT, a co-partner of the Belfast Glass House Company, deed of partnership, 1791. [PRONI.]; in Belfast, 1792. [PRONI.D298.80]

INGLIS, DENNIS, a merchant on board the Ross of Belfast 1689, 1690. [NRS.E72.3.20/21]

INNIS, JOSEPH, in Belfast, co-owner of the Joseph and Mary of Belfast, a bond, 1723. [PRONI.D354.385]; trading with Spain and Gibraltar, 1734, [PRONI.D354.491]; a merchant in Belfast, a lease, 1726. [PRONI.D270.1]

IRVINE, THOMAS, in Belfast, 1669. [PRONI.T307A]

IRWIN, JOHN, a deed of assignation, Rosemary Lane, Belfast, 1791. [PRONI.CR3.32B.8]; a deed, 1795. [PRONI.CR3.32.B.1.9]

IRWIN, WILLIAM, was admitted as a Freeman of Belfast in 1774. [TBB]

ISAAC, JOHN, was admitted as a Freeman of Belfast in 1728. [TBB]

JACKSON, JAMES, son of Nathaniel Jackson a yeoman in Old Park, Belfast, was apprenticed on board the Fidelity of Belfast owned by Robert Andrews and Company in Belfast, in 1718. [PRONI.D354.368A/B]

JACKSON, JOHN, a butcher, was admitted as a Freeman of Belfast in 1726. [TBB]

THE PEOPLE OF BELFAST, 1600-1799

JACKSON, JOHN, master of the Houlikan of Belfast trading with Barbados in 1746. [NRS.E504.34.1]

JACKSON, ROBERT, a glover, was admitted as a Free Commoner of Belfast in 1650. [TBB]

JEFFORD, Lt. Col. Sir JOHN, was admitted as a Free Stapler of Belfast in 1640. [TBB]

JELLY, JOHN, a tailor in Lisbarnett, County Down, was admitted as a Freeman of Belfast in 1730. [TBB]

JERVIS, JOHN, a carpenter, was admitted as a Freeman of Belfast in 1728. [TBB]

JOHNSON, ALEXANDER, a burgess of Belfast, 1639. [TBB]

JOHNSON, JOHN, a burgess of Belfast in 1639. [TBB]

JOHNSTON, ADAM, in Belfast, 1689. [NRS.GD26.13.385]

JOHNSTON, HUGH, a grocer from Belfast, was naturalised in South Carolina in 1798. [NARA.M1183]

JOHNSTON, JAMES, in Belfast, 1669. [PRONI.T307A]

JOHNSTON, JOHN, a husbandman in Belfast, was admitted as a Freeman of Belfast in 1656. [TBB]

JOHNSTON, JOHN, [1], in Belfast, 1669. [PRONI.T307A]

JOHNSTON, JOHN, [2], in Belfast, 1669. [PRONI.T307A]

JOHNSTON, JOHN, a tailor and a Freeman of Belfast in 1673. [TBB]

JOHNSTON, JOHN, in Inverlochy, son of Adam Johnston in Belfast, a letter, 1689. [NRS.GD26.13.385]

JOHNSTON, JOHN, a merchant in Belfast, a deed, 1714. [NRS.RD3.141.75]

THE PEOPLE OF BELFAST, 1600-1799

JOHNSTON, ROBERT, born in Scotland, a merchant in Belfast, and a planter in Antigua, ca. 1690. [CTB.1685-1689.521]

JOHNSTON, WILLIAM, a baker, was admitted as a Freeman of Belfast in 1729. [TBB]; in Belfast, a deed, 1742. [PRONI.D354.364]; a burgess of Belfast, a letter 1754. [PRONI.D354.1007]

JOHNSTON, WILLIAM, a barber, was admitted as a Freeman of Belfast in 1758. [TBB]

JONES, JOHN, an apprentice in Belfast, a letter, 1688. [NRS.GD215.14.185]

JONES, LEWIS, an attorney in Belfast, was admitted as a Freeman of Belfast in 1754. [TBB]

JONES, MOSES, master of the Merchants Adventurers of Belfast trading with Barbados, 1682, [NRS.E72.19.5]; master of the William and John of Belfast 1689, trading with Virginia. [CTB.111.985]

JONES, ROGER, vicar of Belfast Corporation Church in 1666.

JONES, VALENTINE, in Belfast, a lease in Lower Malone, Belfast, in 1770, [PRONI.D509.482]; a lease in High Street, Belfast, in 1780. [PRONI.D509.617]; of Belfast, aged over 80, died in Portpatrick during 1808. [SM.70.879]

JONES, VALENTINE, junior, was admitted as a Freeman of Belfast in 1737. [TBB]

JOY, ANDREW, a mason, was admitted as a Freeman of Belfast in 1729. [TBB]

JOY, FRANCIS, founder of the 'Belfast News Letter', 1737. [TBB]

THE PEOPLE OF BELFAST, 1600-1799

JOY, GEORGE, was admitted as a Freeman of Belfast in 1777. [TBB]

JOY, HENRY, a merchant in Belfast, witness to the will of Thomas McIlwain, 1777.

JOY, HENRY, jr., was admitted as a Freeman of Belfast in 1777. [TBB]

JOY, HENRY, born 1754, son of Robert Joy and his wife Grace Rainey, grandson of Francis Joy and his wife Margaret Martin of the Lodge, Belfast, died 1835, his wife Mary Isabella Holmes, daughter of John Holmes, a banker in Belfast, and his wife Isabella Patterson, born 1771, died 1832. [New Burying Ground MI]

JOY, RICHARD, a chandler, was admitted as a Freeman of Belfast in 1728. [TBB]

JOY, ROBERT, a cotton spinner in Belfast, 1777. [TBB]

JOY, MCCABE, and MCCRACKEN, in Belfast, a letter, 1783. [PRONI.D207.28.553]

KEAN, PATRICK, a servant, was admitted as a Freeman of Belfast in 1730. [TBB]

KEAS, WILLIAM, a butcher in Belfast, was admitted as a Freeman of Belfast in 1760. [TBB]

KELLIE, JAMES, master of the Marie of Belfast 1684. [NRS.E72.19.9]

KELSO, HAMILTON, only son of Henry Kelso a merchant in Belfast, matriculated at Glasgow University in 1758, graduated MD in 1762. [MAGU.58]

KELSO, ..., of Lisburn, a merchant, was admitted as a Freeman of Belfast in 1729. [TBB]

THE PEOPLE OF BELFAST, 1600-1799

KEMP, RONALD, a merchant in Belfast, died in Comrie, was admitted as a Freeman of Belfast in 1727. [TBB]

KENDAL, LEONARD, was admitted as a Freeman of Belfast in 1725. [TBB]

KENIAN, DANIEL, was admitted as a Freeman of Belfast in 1727. [TBB]

KENITYE, JOHN, a boatman, was admitted as a Free Commoner of Belfast in 1654. [TBB]

KENLEY, JAMES, in Belfast, lease of Lower Malone, Belfast, in 1770. [PRONI.D509.485]

KENNEDY, ALEXANDER, born in Belfast, took the Oath of Allegiance to King Charles II in 1672.

KENNEDY, ARTHUR, a merchant, was admitted as a Freeman of Belfast in 1733. [TBB]

KENNEDY, CHARLES, a cutler, was admitted as a Freeman of Belfast in 1736. [TBB]

KENNEDY, GILBERT, a Presbyterian minister in Belfast from 1744, died 1773. [HM]

KENNEDY, HELEN, daughter of David Kennedy a surgeon in Edinburgh, spouse of James Chalmers in Belfast, a deed, 1671, [NRS.RD2.30.319]

KENNEDY, HUGH, was admitted as a Freeman of Belfast in 1733. [TBB]

KENNEDY, JAMES TRAILL, a co-partner of the Belfast Glass House Company, deed of partnership, 1791. [PRONI.]

KENNEDY, JOHN, a blacksmith, was admitted as a Free Commoner of Belfast in 1647. [TBB]

THE PEOPLE OF BELFAST, 1600-1799

KENNEDY, JOSEPH, master of the New Draper of Belfast in 1793. [NRS.E504.4.10]

KENNEDY, SAMUEL, a mariner from Belfast, was naturalised in South Carolina in 1797. [NARA.M1183]

KENNEDY, THOMAS, in Belfast, 1669. [PRONI.T307A]

KENNEDY, WILLIAM, in Belfast, 1669. [PRONI.T307A]

KENNEDY, WILLIAM, a cooper, was admitted as a Freeman of Belfast in 1731. [TBB]

KENNEDY, WILLIAM, a farmer in Knocknagony, was admitted as a Freeman of Belfast in 1737. [TBB]

KENNEDY, ..., in the barony of Belfast, 1659. [C]

KENNEDY, THOMAS, in Belfast, 1669. [PRONI.T307A]

KENNING, THOMAS, born 1768, died 1816, husband of Jane, ..., born 1775, died 1801. [New Burying Ground MI, Belfast]

KERR, JOHN, a farmer, was admitted as a Freeman of Belfast in 1728. [TBB]

KERRAN, THOMAS, a burgess of Belfast, 1639. [TBB]

KILBEE, ELLEN, second daughter of James Kilbee in Belfast, married Robert Stuart a merchant in Glasgow, there in 1815. [SM.77.873]

KILPATRICK, BARBARA, in Belfast, 1669. [PRONI.T307A]

KILPATRICK, JOHN, in Belfast, 1669. [PRONI.T307A]

KILPATRICK, ROBERT, in Belfast, 1669. [PRONI.T307A]

KINARD, WILLIAM, in Belfast in 1645. [TBB]

THE PEOPLE OF BELFAST, 1600-1799

KING, ANDREW, an adventurer who was granted land in the north-east quarter of the barony of Belfast, 1643. [SPI.1642-1659: 354]

KING, MATTHEW, a merchant in Belfast, a deed, 1697. [NRS.RD4.81.859]

KING, ROBERT, a Scot in Belfast, to be transported to the west of Ireland in 1653. [TBB]

KINKEAD, JOHN, was admitted as a Freeman of Belfast in 1728. [TBB]

KINKEAD, MOSES, was admitted as a Freeman of Belfast in 1728. [TBB]

KINNAN, DENNIS, a carman, was admitted as a Freeman of Belfast in 1730. [TBB]

KIRK, WILLIAM, a saddler, was admitted as a Freeman of Belfast in 1728. [TBB]

KIRKER, WILLIAM, of the Falls, was admitted as a Freeman of Belfast in 1771. [TBB]

KIRKLAND, WILLIAM, born 1789, a mariner from Belfast, was naturalised in South Carolina in 1807. [NARA.M1183]

KIRKPATRICK, HENRY, a merchant in Belfast, was admitted as a Freeman of Belfast in 1760. [TBB]

KIRKPATRICK, HUGH, a merchant in Belfast, a deed, 1687. [NRS.RD2.68.95]

KIRKPATRICK, Reverend JAMES, in Belfast, a letter, 1723. [PRONI.D354.629]

KIRKPATRICK, JAMES, born 1761, died 1823, husband of Rosina ......, born 1781, died 1816. [New Burying Ground MI]

KIRKPATRICK, SAMUEL, a stay-maker, was admitted as a Freeman of Belfast in 1731. [TBB]

KIRKPATRICK, THOMAS, a smith, was admitted as a Freeman of Belfast in 1731. [TBB]

KIRKPATRICK, WILLIAM, a surgeon in Belfast, a deed, 1687. [NRS.RD4.60.565]

KIRKWOOD, JOHN, master of the Ross of Belfast 1689. [NRS.E72.3.19]; master of the Mary of Belfast 1689. [NRS.E72.3.14]

KIRKWOOD, WILLIAM, of the Falls, was admitted as a Freeman of Belfast in 1771. [TBB]

KIRKWOOD, WILLIAM, jr., of the Falls, was admitted as a Freeman of Belfast in 1771. [TBB]

KNOUCLES, PETER, the Customs Collector at Belfast, 1691. [RPCS.XVI.310]

KNOX, JOHN, a watchmaker, was admitted as a Freeman of Belfast in 1729. [TBB]

KNOX, ROBERT, born 1749, died 1837. [New Burying Ground MI]

KNOX, THOMAS, a merchant from Glasgow who settled in Belfast by 1669, was admitted as a burgess of Glasgow from 1680 to 1697, died 1728. [PRONI.D235.4]; he was admitted as a burgess of Belfast in 1680, [TBB]; a merchant in Belfast, deeds, 1684, 1691-1692. [NRS.GD109.2749/3828; RD3.78.304; RD2.72.833]; he was admitted as a burgess and guilds-brother of Ayr in 1695. [ABR]; husband of Bessie Spang; a burgess 1669-1680. [BMF]

KYLE, HUGH, an innkeeper in Belfast, was admitted as a Freeman of Belfast in 1774. [TBB]

THE PEOPLE OF BELFAST, 1600-1799

KYLE, JOHN, master of the Jean of Belfast trading with Madeira in 1691. [NRS.E72.19.22]

LAIRD, MARGARET, born 1759, daughter of Reverend William Laird, died 1831. [New Burying Ground MI]

LAITHAM, JOHN, born 1768, died 1816. [New Burying Ground MI]

LAMOND, JOHN, master of the Blessing of Belfast in 1666-1667, master of the Salmon of Belfast in 1667. [NRS.E72.3.1/2; E72.10.1]

LANE, JOHN, a clothier, was admitted as a Freeman of Belfast in 1635. [TBB]

LANGFORD, Sir HERCULES, a gentleman and burgess of Belfast from 1669 until 1680. [BMF]

LANGTREE, JOHN, was admitted as a Free Stapler of Belfast in 1625. [TBB]

LARKHAM, HENRY, a weaver, was admitted as a Freeman of Belfast in 1638. [TBB]

LAWE, JOHN, a merchant, was admitted as a Freeman of Belfast in 1639. [TBB]

LAW, SAMUEL, a dealer, was admitted as a Freeman of Belfast in 1783. [TBB]

LEATHER, DAVID, in Belfast, a lease in Skipper's Lane, Belfast, 1767. [PRONI.D238.54]

LEITHES, ADAM, was admitted as a Freeman of Belfast in 1640. [TBB]

LEITHES, HUGH, a glover, was admitted as a Freeman of Belfast in 1639. [TBB]

THE PEOPLE OF BELFAST, 1600-1799

LEATHES, JOHN, eldest son of William Leithes, a merchant, was admitted as a Free Stapler of Belfast in 1639. [TBB]; a burgess 1634-1667. [BMF]

LEATHES, JOHN jr., a merchant burgess 1646-1693. [BMF]

LEATHES, MOSES, master of the Speedwell of Belfast 1689. [NRS.E72.3.19]

LEATHES, ROBERT, a burgess 1669-1717. [BMF]

LEATHES, WILLIAM, a merchant, was admitted as a burgess of Belfast in 1640. [TBB]; a merchant burgess 1642-1660. [BMF]

LEBYRTT, ROBERT, in Belfast, lease in Castle Street, Belfast, 1717. [PRONI.D509.44]

LEE, WILLIAM, in Belfast, lease of the Course in Belfast, in 1770. [PRONI.D509.495]

LEGGE, BENJAMIN, a merchant, was admitted as a Freeman of Belfast in 1727. [TBB]; a merchant in Belfast, trading with Spain and Gibraltar, 1734. [PRONI.D354.493]

LENARD, BRYAN, a slater, was admitted as a Freeman of Belfast in 1726. [TBB]

LENNOX, JOHN, in Belfast, 1669. [PRONI. T307A]

LENNOX, MARTHA, in Belfast, a lease, 1731. [PRONI.D270.3]

LENNOX, ROBERT, a merchant in Belfast, 1676, and a yeoman there in 1678, bonds. [NRS.GD10.819/823]; born 1661, a merchant in Belfast, died 1733. [Old Poorhouse MI, Belfast]

THE PEOPLE OF BELFAST, 1600-1799

LENNOX, ROBERT, a lease in Rosemary Lane, Belfast, 1723. [PRONI.CR3.32.B.1.4]; a merchant in Belfast, a lease, 1731, [PRONI.D270.3]

LENNOX, SAMUEL, in Belfast, a bond, 1676. [NRS.GD10.819]

LESLIE, WILLIAM, a gentleman in Belfast, 1659. [C]

LE SQUIRE, HENRY, a burgess of Belfast in 1635, 1642. [TBB]

LE SQUIRE, Mrs, in Belfast in 1645. [TBB]

LEVITT, Captain THOMAS, master of the <u>Charles of Belfast</u> was admitted as a burgess and guilds-brother of Edinburgh in 1701. [EBR]

LEWIS, ALEXANDER, son of the Sovereign, was admitted as a Freeman of Belfast in 1774. [TBB]

LEWIS, CHARLES, son of the Sovereign, was admitted as a Freeman of Belfast in 1774. [TBB]

LEWIS, JAMES, in Belfast, a lease, 1770. [PRONI.D509.423]; Sovereign by 1783. [TBB]

LEWIS, JAMES, son of the Sovereign, was admitted as a Freeman of Belfast in 1774. [TBB]

LEWIS, JOHN, a carpenter, was admitted as a Freeman of Belfast in 1728. [TBB]

LEYTHE, JOHN, a gentleman, was admitted as a burgess of Belfast in 1642. [TBB]; in Belfast in 1659. [C]

LEYTHES, PETER, born 1633, from Belfast, a sailor aboard the <u>Success of London</u>, bound via the Canary Islands for New England in 1657, captured by a Dutch privateer on return voyage. [TNA.HCA.Exams.74:3-11.Jan.1662]

THE PEOPLE OF BELFAST, 1600-1799

LEYTHE, WILLIAM, a gentleman, was admitted as a burgess of Belfast in 1639, 1642. [TBB]

LIGHTFOOT, THOMAS, a tailor, was admitted as a Free Commoner of Belfast in 1650. [TBB]

LIGGAT, JAMES, in Belfast, surrender of a lease, 1779. [PRONI.D509.598]

LINDEN, JANE, born 1787, daughter of Matthew Linden, died 1807. [New Burying Ground MI]

LINDEN, MATTHEW, born 1761, died 1837. [New Burying Ground MI]

LINDSAY, JAMES, a merchant, was admitted as a Free Merchant Stapler of Belfast in 1644. [TBB]

LINDSAY, JOHN, a farmer, was admitted as a Freeman of Belfast in 1728. [TBB]

LINDSAY, ROBERT, a farmer, was admitted as a Freeman of Belfast in 1728. [TBB]

LITTLE, JOHN, in Belfast, lease of Upper Malone, Belfast, 1770. [PRONI.D509.496]

LOCKHART, ALEXANDER, a Scot in Belfast, to be transported to the west of Ireland in 1653. [TBB]

LOCKHART, WILLIAM, a merchant, was admitted as a burgess of Belfast in 1687, [TBB]; in Belfast, a lease, 1688. [PRONI.D412.1]; a merchant burgess 1687-1698. [BMF]

LOCHHEAD, JOHN, a laborer, was admitted as a Freeman of Belfast in 1658. [TBB]

LOGAN, CHARLES, of the Falls, was admitted as a Freeman of Belfast in 1771. [TBB]

THE PEOPLE OF BELFAST, 1600-1799

LOGAN, EDWARD, a yeoman in Belfast, witness to the will of James Smith, probate 1720, Dublin.

LOGAN, JOHN, in Belfast, 1669. [PRONI.T307A]

LOGAN, NANCY, in Belfast, 1669. [PRONI.T307A]

LOGAN, WILLIAM, in Belfast, lease of Ballygomatin in Belfast, 1770. [PRONI.D509.500]

LOGAN, ……, in the barony of Belfast, 1659. [C]

LONGE, DAVID, a butcher, was admitted as a Free Commoner of Belfast in 1649. [TBB]

LONG, GEORGE, a gardener, was admitted as a Freeman of Belfast in 1729. [TBB]

LORIMER, JOHN, a shipmaster in Belfast, a deed, 1684. [NRS.RD2.63.217]; master of the Providence of Belfast trading with Montserrat in 1686. [NRS.E72.12.13]

LOVE, JOHN, a burgess of Belfast, 1639. [TBB]

LOWRY, HUGH, a cooper, was admitted as a Freeman of Belfast in 1728. [TBB]

LOWRY, JAMES, of the Falls, was admitted as a Freeman of Belfast in 1771. [TBB]

LUDFORD, JOHN, a burgess 1757. [BMF]

LUGSTON, WILLIAM, in Belfast, 1643. [TBB]

LUKE, JAMES, and his wife Catherine, in Belfast, parents of Campbell who died in Philadelphia in 1820, and William who died in New York in 1837. [Belfast MI]

LUKE, JOHN, born 1733, a merchant in Belfast, died 1822. [New Burying Ground MI]

THE PEOPLE OF BELFAST, 1600-1799

LUKE, NINIAN, a merchant aboard the Joan of Belfast trading with Madeira in 1691. [NRS.E72.19.22]

LUSK, ROBERT, master of the Chichester of Belfast, from Belfast to Virginia in1745. [VaGaz.466]

LYLE, JOHN, a merchant in Belfast, trading with Cadiz, a letter, 1729. [PRONI.D354.631]

LYLE, THOMAS, master of the Hanover of Belfast 1738. [TNA.CO5.510]; master of the Grace and Molly of Belfast trading with Barbados in 1748. [NRS.E504.28.3]

LYNDON, ROGER, a burgess of Belfast in 1646. [TBB]

LYONS, DAVID, a yeoman, was admitted as a Freeman of Belfast in 1725. [TBB]

LYONS, DAVID, a lease of Old Park in Belfast, 1770. [PRONI.D509.496]

LYONS, HENRY, in Belfast, a lease, 1777. [PRONI.D509.576]

LYON, JACOB, a farmer, was admitted as a Freeman of Belfast in 1728. [TBB]

LYON, JOHN, master of the James of Belfast 1685-1686. [NRS.E72.12.9/12]

LYONS, THOMAS, in Belfast, a lease in 1770. [PRONI.D509.498]

LYONS, WILLIAM, a linen draper in Belfast, was admitted as a Freeman of Belfast in 1773. [TBB]

LYTHOM, WILLIAM, a glazier, was admitted as a Freeman of Belfast in 1639. [TBB]

MCADAM, THOMAS, a merchant in Belfast, was admitted as a Freeman of Belfast in 1773. [TBB]

THE PEOPLE OF BELFAST, 1600-1799

MCAFEE, AGNES, born 1784, a spinster from Belfast, bound for Philadelphia aboard the Commerce in 1804. [BL.Addl.ms]

MCALEXANDER, ROBERT, a weaver, was admitted as a Freeman of Belfast in 1728. [TBB]

MCALLISTER, ALEXANDER, a carrier, was admitted as a Freeman of Belfast in 1731. [TBB]

MCALLISTER, DANIEL, a farmer, was admitted as a Freeman of Belfast in 1729. [TBB]

MCALLISTER, DAVID, in Belfast, 1669. [PRONO.T307A]

MCALISTER, JOHN, in Belfast, 1769. [NRS.B82.1.15/2]

MCADAM, JAMES, in Belfast, a letter, 1793. [PRONI.D530.22]

MCADAM, Mrs JANE, in Belfast, a letter, 1801. [PRONI.D530.22]

MCBRIDE, DAVID, a merchant in Belfast, was admitted as a burgess and guilds-brother of Ayr in 1715. [ABR]

MCBRIDE, JOHN, a merchant, was admitted Free Stapler and Commoner of Belfast, in 1644. [TBB249]

MCBRIDE, JOHN, Presbyterian minister at Rosemary Church, Belfast, in 1694, died in Belfast 1718. [F.VII.531]; a preacher in Belfast, was admitted as a burgess and guilds-brother of Glasgow in 1704, [GBR]; in Belfast, letters, 1704-1709, [NRS.CH1.5.6.186/190]; in Belfast, 1718. [IWD]

MCBRIDE, JOHN, master of the Mercury of Belfast 1764. [TNA.CO106.1]

MCCAAL, HUGH, a tailor, was admitted as a Freeman of Belfast in 1726. [TBB]

THE PEOPLE OF BELFAST, 1600-1799

MCCABE, THOMAS, a cotton spinner in Belfast, 1777. [TBB]; a co-partner of the Belfast Glass House Company, deed of partnership, 1791. [PRONI.]

MCCABE, Mrs MARY, born 1717, died 1801. [New Burying Ground MI]

MCCAGHAN, ARCHIBALD, a burgess of Belfast in 1639. [TBB]

MCCALL, DAVID, a tailor, was admitted as a Freeman of Belfast in 1725. [TBB]

MCCANCE, JOHN, in Belfast, a lease, 1770. [PRONI.D509.501]

MCCANN, ARTHUR, a baker, was admitted as a Freeman of Belfast in 1730. [TBB]

MCCARTNEY, AGNES, born 1728, from Belfast, a Jacobite in 1745-1746, captured at Carlisle and transported in chains to the American Plantations. [P.III.23]

MCCARTNEY, ARTHUR, son of the late George McCartney, a merchant who was admitted as a burgess of Belfast in 1691. [TBB]; a merchant burgess 1691-1706. [BMF]

MACARTNEY, CHARLES, a tailor, was admitted as a Freeman of Belfast in 1752. [TBB]

MACCARTNEY, GEORGE, a merchant, was admitted as a Free Commoner of Belfast in 1651, [TBB]; in Belfast, a deed, 1667, [NRS.RD2.19.361]; letters some re trade with the West Indies, 1660-1667, [PRONI.MIC.19.1]; 1668 [ActsPCCol.755/1041]; in Belfast 1669, [PRONI.T307A]; deeds, 1674, 1679. [NRS.RH15.91.60]; a letter, 1680, [SPDom.1680.455]; a deed, 1697, [NRS.RD2.80/2.672]

THE PEOPLE OF BELFAST, 1600-1799

MCCARTNEY, Captain GEORGE, was admitted as a burgess of Belfast in 1659. [TBB]; a merchant burgess 1659-1691. [BMF]

MACCARTNEY, GEORGE, a merchant in Belfast, High Sheriff of County Antrim in 1681, [UJA.11.1.79]; 1690. [NRS.E72.3.20]; 1691, [RPCS.xvi.309]; the Member of Parliament for Belfast in the Irish Parliament in 1692, [TBB.231]; probate 1694, PCC

MCCARTNEY, GEORGE, a merchant in Belfast, was admitted as a burgess and guilds-brother of Ayr in 1697, [ABR]; was admitted as a burgess of Belfast in 1702. [TBB]; a gentleman burgess 1702-1757. [BMF]

MCCARTNEY, GEORGE, in Belfast, 1731. [NRS.GD10.479]; a burgess of Belfast, a letter 1754. [PRONI.D354.1007]; son of the Sovereign, was admitted as a Freeman of Belfast in 1756. [TBB]

MACCARTNEY, ISAAC, a merchant in Belfast, was admitted as a burgess of Aberdeen in 1696. [ABR]; was admitted as a burgess of Belfast in 1701. [TBB]; a deed, 1715; 1722. [NRS.RD2.105.77; AC9.849]; owner of the brigantine Ann of Belfast bound for Bremen and Hamburg, Germany, charter party, 1723. [PRONI.D354.381]; 1728, [NRS.NRAS.631/4, bundle A903]; letters 1727-1731, [NRS.GD10.1421.11.462/479]; a lease. 1732. [PRONI.D199.1]; a merchant burgess 1701-1707. [BMF]; letter book, 1704-1706. [PRONI.D501]

MACCARTNEY, Sir JAMES, was admitted as a burgess of Belfast in 1676, [TBB]; in Belfast, lease of Old Park, Belfast, 1692. [PRONI.D509.30]; a lawyer burgess, 1676-1715. [BMF]

MCCARTNEY, JAMES, a butcher, was admitted as a Freeman of Belfast in 1726. [TBB]

THE PEOPLE OF BELFAST, 1600-1799

MCCARTNEY, JAMES, was born 1693 in Belfast, son of James McCartney a judge of the Queen's Bench in Ireland, a student at Trinity College, Dublin, in 1710, graduated LL.D. in 1718, [AD]; was admitted as a burgess of Belfast in 1717. [TBB]; Member of Parliament for Belfast in the Irish Parliament, 1692, 1695. [TBB.231]

MCCARTNEY, JOHN, a weaver, was admitted as a Freeman of Belfast in 1674. [TBB]

MCCARTNEY, JOSEPH, son of the Sovereign, was admitted as a Freeman of Belfast in 1761. [TBB]

MCCARTNEY, WILLIAM, in Belfast, a lease in Broad Street, Belfast, 1746. [PRONI.D298.12/13]

MCCARTNEY, WILLIAM, Member of Parliament for Belfast, 1752-1757. [PRONI.T2873.2]; son of the Sovereign, was admitted as a Freeman of Belfast in 1756. [TBB]

MCCAY, FREDERICK, in Belfast, a letter, 1704. [PRONI.D1582]

MCCLAINE, WILLIAM, master of the *William of Belfast* 1683. [NRS.E72.3.12]

MCCLEAN, JOHN, a tailor, was admitted as a Freeman of Belfast in 1731. [TBB]

MCCLEAN, WILLIAM, in Belfast, a lease, 1787. [PRONI.D199.13]

MCCLEARY, ANDREW, a tailor, was admitted as a Freeman of Belfast in 1731. [TBB]

MCCLEARY, WILLIAM, a baker, was admitted as a Freeman of Belfast in 1731. [TBB]

THE PEOPLE OF BELFAST, 1600-1799

MCCLEERY, Mrs JANE, born 1751, daughter of John Hay a bookseller, died 1830. [New Burying Ground MI]

MCCLELLAND, RICHARD, born 1761, died 1807, husband of Tabitha ….., born 1768, died 1844. [New Burying Ground MI]

MCCLELAND, …….., in the barony of Belfast, 1659. [C]

MCCLENAGHAN, JOHN, born 1793 in Belfast, applied for naturalisation in Marion district, South Carolina, in 1823. [NARA.M1183]

MCCLUNE, NOAH, a barber in Belfast, was admitted as a Freeman of Belfast in 1760. [TBB]

MCCLUNEY, ROBERT, born 1768, a surgeon, died 1837. [New Burying Ground MI]

MCCLUNEY, WILLIAM, was admitted as a Freeman of Belfast in 1736. [TBB]

MCCLURE, ARCHIBALD, was admitted as a Freeman of Belfast in 1777. [TBB]

MCCLURE, JOHN, a carman, was admitted as a Freeman of Belfast in 1739. [TBB]

MCCLURE, ROBERT WATT, lease of Graham's Entry, Belfast, in 1796. [PRONI.D298.91]

MCCLURE, WILLIAM, born 1757, died 1843, husband of Elizabeth ….., born 1773, died1848. [New Burying Ground MI]

MCCOMB, HERCULES, a ship carpenter in Belfast, was admitted as a Freeman of Belfast in 1773. [TBB]

MCCOMB, THOMAS, born 1762, a merchant in Belfast, died 1820, husband of Elizabeth Hudson, born 1772, died 1842. [New Burying Ground MI]

THE PEOPLE OF BELFAST, 1600-1799

MCCONNELL, ALEXANDER, master of the Hopewell of Belfast 1771. [NRS.E504.4.5]

MCCONNELL, JOHN, born 1754 in Belfast, a tailor and an indentured servant, absconded from his master in Delaware in 1774. [PaGaz:9.2.1774]

MCCONNELL, JOHN, in Belfast, a bond, 1790. [PRONI.D491.38]

MCCONNELL, WILLIAM, born 1770, died 1844, husband of Margaret ……., born 1784, died 1842. [New Burying Ground MI, Belfast[

MCCONNOCHIE, JAMES, master of the James of Belfast 1695. [NRS.E72.19.23]

MCCORMICK, DONNELL, a shoemaker, was admitted as a Free Commoner of Belfast in 1649. [TBB]

MCCORMICK, EDWARD, master of the Isaac of Belfast 1729-1735. [PRONI.D354.475]; master of the Swift of Belfast trading with Jamaica in 1743, [NRS.E504.28.1]; master of the Oliver of Belfast trading with Antigua and Barbados in 1770-1772. [NRS.E504.15.18; E504.4.5]

MCCORMACK, JOHN, a merchant in Belfast, aboard the Content of Belfast trading with France in 1681. [SPDom.1681.228]

MCCORMICK, JOHN, master of the Martha of Belfast, in 1749. [NRS.E504.4.1]

MCCORMACK, Corporal THOMAS, a Scot in Belfast, to be transported to the west of Ireland in 1653. [TBB]

MCCORRY, BRIAN, a burgess of Belfast in 1639. [TBB]

MCCRACKEN, ANDREW, in Belfast, a bond, 1790. [PRONI.D491.38]

THE PEOPLE OF BELFAST, 1600-1799

MCCRACKEN, HENRY JOY, born 1767, executed 1798. [New Burying Ground MI]

MCCRACKEN, HUGH, in Belfast, 1798. [PRONI.D272.35A]

MCCRACKEN, JOHN, was admitted as a Freeman of Belfast in 1643. [TBB]

MCCRACKEN, JOHN, a lease of Rosemary Lane, Belfast, 1791. [PRONI.CR3.32B.1.8]; a deed, 1795. [PRONI.CR3.B.1.9]

MCCRACKEN, Captain, founder of the Belfast Ropeworks Company in 1758. [TBB]

MCCRAIGHT, JOHN, an apothecary, was admitted as a Freeman of Belfast in 1731. [TBB]

MCCRAE, ALEXANDER, a merchant in Belfast, deeds, 1699. [NRS.RD2.83.285/461; RD4.85/79/859/953/954]

MCCRAE, JOHN, a seaman from Belfast, to be released from Edinburgh or Canongate tollbooth in July 1689. [RPCS.XIII.554]

MCCREA, WILLIAM, a weaver, was admitted as a Freeman of Belfast in 1727. [TBB]

MCCREE, ALEXANDER, a merchant in Belfast, a deed, 1714. [NRS.RD4.89.589]

MCCREARY, JAMES, a butcher in Belfast, was admitted as a Freeman of Belfast in 1760. [TBB]

MCCREE, JAMES, in Belfast, apprentice on board the James and Ellice of Belfast owned by Daniel Mussenden, 1720. [PRONI.D354.372]

MCCREEDY, JOHN, born 1726, late of Downpatrick, died in Belfast in 1806. [New Burying Ground MI]

THE PEOPLE OF BELFAST, 1600-1799

MCCREERY, JOHN, a tailor, was admitted as a Freeman of Belfast in 1725. [TBB]

MCCREERY, ..., in the barony of Belfast, 1659. [C]

MCCRONE, or GAW, MARGERY, an heir of Patrick Gaw in Belfast, 1792. [PRONI.D298.80]

MCCUARY, GEORGE, a mason, was admitted as a Freeman of Belfast in 1731. [TBB]

MCCULLOCH, Captain JAMES, a merchant in Belfast, owner of the Mary of Belfast a galley, bound for Barbados, 1726. [NRS.AC32.116-213; AC9.967]

MCCULLOCH, JOHN, was admitted as a Free Stapler of Belfast in 1638. [TBB.246]

MCCULLOUGH, JOHN, born 1778, died 1830, husband of Elizabeth ......, born 1785, died 1847. [Shankill MI, Belfast]

MCCUTCHEON, ADAM, a merchant in Belfast, will, probate 1718, Dublin. Reference to his children Thomas, Jean, Isabel, and Margaret, his brother James and his children, his sister ....Craig and her son Archibald Craig, his brother in law Archibald Craig, his brother in law Robert Allan, Joseph Innes, William Stevenson, witnesses Reverend Samuel Ross in Londonderry, James White a cooper in Belfast, and John Hamilton apprentice to William Stevenson.

MCCUTCHEON, JOHN, born 1775, an architect and builder in Belfast, died 1822 in London. [New Burying Ground MI]

MCDONALD, JAMES, son of the Town Sergeant, was admitted as a Freeman of Belfast in 1758. [TBB]

THE PEOPLE OF BELFAST, 1600-1799

MCDONALD, JOHN, son of the Town Sergeant, was admitted as a Freeman of Belfast in 1758. [TBB]

MCDONALD, JOHN, master of the Ann of Belfast in 1776. [NRS.E504.15.26]

MCDONNELL, ALEXANDER, a gentleman in Belfast, 1659. [C]

MCDONNELL, ALEXANDER, born 1776, died 1831, husband of Elisabeth Mary ....., born 1774, died 1849. [New Burying Ground MI]

MCDONNELL, DONNELL, a gentleman in Belfast, 1659. [C]

MCDONNELL, JAMES, a bricklayer, was admitted as a Freeman of Belfast in 1731. [TBB]

MCDOUGALL, JAMES, a merchant in Belfast, was admitted as a Freeman of Belfast in 1748. [TBB]

MCDONNELL, JAMES, of Murleagh, County Antrim, born 1763, a physician in Belfast, died in 1845, husband of (1) Eliza, daughter of John Clark in Belfast, who died in 1798, aand (2) Penelope, daughter of James Montgomery in Larne, who died in 1851. [Layde, Cushenall MI, County Antrim]

MCDOWAL, ALEXANDER, a mariner from Belfast, was naturalised in South Carolina in 1796. [NARA.M1183]

MCDOWAL, GEORGE, in Belfast, 1669. [PRONI.T307A]

MCDOWELL, JOHN, a merchant, was admitted as a Merchant Stapler and Free Commoner of Belfast in 1645. [TBB]

MCDOWELL, JOHN, a seaman from Belfast, to be released from Edinburgh or Canongate tollbooth in July 1689. [RPCS.XIII.554]

THE PEOPLE OF BELFAST, 1600-1799

MCDOWALL, JOHN, a lease in North Street, Belfast, in 1778. [PRONI.D278.47]

MCDOWELL, ROBERT, a farmer, was admitted as a Freeman of Belfast in 1728. [TBB]

MCDOWELL, ROBERT, a baker, was admitted as a Freeman of Belfast in 1746. [TBB]

MCDOWELL, WILLIAM, a fiddler, was admitted as a Freeman of Belfast in 1728. [TBB]

MCELROY, ANDREW, in Belfast in 1645. [TBB]

MCELWEE, JOHN, a merchant in Belfast in 1754. [PRONI.D509.63]

MCELWRATH, JAMES, a burgess of Belfast, a letter 1754. [PRONI.D354.1007]

MCELRATH, WILLIAM, a shopkeeper, was admitted as a Freeman of Belfast in 1729. [TBB]

MCEWAN, THOMAS, master of the *Martha of Belfast* in 1747. [NRS.E504.4.1]

MCFADDEN, ARCHIBALD, born 1766, died 1811, husband of Ann ....., born 1771, died 1816. [New Burying Ground MI]

MCFADDEN, HENRY, a perrywig-maker, was admitted as a Freeman of Belfast in 1725. [TBB]

MCFARLING, WILLIAM, of the Falls, was admitted as a Freeman of Belfast in 1771. [TBB]

MCFARRAN, ANDREW, a tailor, was admitted as a Freeman of Belfast in 1746. [TBB]

MCGAHAN, HENRY, a butcher, was admitted as a Freeman of Belfast in 1783. [TBB]

THE PEOPLE OF BELFAST, 1600-1799

MCGARRAGH, GILBERT, was admitted as a Freeman of Belfast in 1641. [TBB]

MAGEE, GEORGE, at Milewater, was admitted as a Freeman of Belfast in 1730. [TBB]

MAGEE, HUGH, a porter in Belfast, was admitted as a Freeman of Belfast in 1730. [TBB]

MAGEE, HUGH, a porter in Belfast, was admitted as a Freeman of Belfast in 1737. [TBB]

MCGEE, JAMES, born 1678, son of James McGee in Ballyrobert [1634-1714], a merchant in Belfast, died 1703. [New Burying Ground MI]

MAGEE, JAMES, printer of the 'Belfast Courant', 1745. [TBB]

MAGEE, JOSEPH, in Belfast, a lease of Millfield in Belfast, in 1794. [PRONI.D298.87]

MCGEE, NATHANIEL, master of the Margaret and Mary of Belfast 1739, trading with South Carolina. [TNA.CO5.510]

MAGEE, ROBERT, a farmer, was admitted as a Freeman of Belfast in 1728. [TBB]

MAGEE, ROBERT, a cooper in Belfast, was admitted as a Freeman of Belfast in 1737. [TBB]

MAGEE, ROBERT, born 1783, died 1857, husband of Hannah …., born 1789, died 1841. [Shankill MI, Belfast]

MAGEE, WILLIAM, in Belfast, a bond, 1790. [PRONI.D491.50]

MCGIE, JAMES, a gentleman in Belfast, was admitted as a burgess and guilds-brother of Glasgow in 1677. [GBR]

THE PEOPLE OF BELFAST, 1600-1799

MCGILL, JOHN, master of the Joan of Belfast 1681. [NRS.E72.19.5]

MCGOWAN, JOHN, a shoemaker, was admitted as a Free Commoner of Belfast in 1654. [TBB]; in Belfast in 1669. [PRONI.T307A]

MCHERON, JOHN, a seaman from Belfast, to be released from Edinburgh or Canongate tollbooth in July 1689. [RPCS.XIII.554]

MCHOOLE, ALEXANDER, a merchant, was admitted as a Freeman of Belfast in 1658. [TBB.249]

MCHUTCHEON, WILLIAM, master of the Friends Adventure of Belfast in 1686, and of the William and Joan of Belfast in 1689. [NRS.E72.12.13/15]

MCILROTH, Mrs, born 1728, relict of Colonel McIlroth, died in Belfast during 1821. [SM.88.620]

MCILROY, WILLIAM, a huckster, was admitted as a Freeman of Belfast in 1728. [TBB]

MCILVEAN, GILBERT, in Belfast, a lease of Shankill Road, Belfast, 1770, [PRONI.D509.568]; a lease of Rosemary Lane, Belfast, 1787. [PRONI.CR3.32.B1.7]

MCILVEAN, HUGH, a merchant in Belfast, was admitted as a Freeman there in 1774. [TBB]; executor for his father Thomas McIlwain in 1777; a lease in Millfield, Belfast, 1790. [PRONI.D296.74]

MCILWAIN, THOMAS, a merchant in Bridge Street, Belfast, father of Mary mother of Ann, Elizabeth and Rebecca; a bond, 1767, [PRONI.D298.32]; father of Hugh McIlwain a merchant in Belfast, probate 1777, Dublin.

THE PEOPLE OF BELFAST, 1600-1799

MCKALL, JOHN, an ale-seller, was admitted as a Freeman of Belfast in 1726. [TBB]

MCKARTINE, JOHN, master of the William and Mary of Belfast in 1691. [NRS.E72.12.18]

MACKAY, COLIN CAMPBELL, of Bighouse, was admitted as a master of the Orange Lodge in Belfast in 1798. [NRS.GD87.2.24]

MACKAY, JAMES, born 1787, eldest son of Alexander Mackay, publisher of the *Belfast Newsletter*, died in 1806. [SM.69.78]

MCKEALE, JOHN, a tailor, was admitted as a Freeman of Belfast in 1731. [TBB]

MCKEE, NEVIN, in Belfast, a lease, 1778. [PRONI.D509.587]

MCKEE, ROBERT, a laborer, was admitted as a Freeman of Belfast in 1658. [TBB]

MCKELVY, HUGH, in Larne, was admitted as a Freeman of Belfast in 1737. [TBB]

MCKELVEY, JOHN, a distiller in Belfast, was admitted as a Freeman of Belfast in 1761. [TBB]

MCKELVEY, SAMUEL, an ale-seller, was admitted as a Freeman of Belfast in 1725. [TBB]

MCKENIE, JOHN, a seaman from Belfast, to be released from Edinburgh or Canongate tollbooth in July 1689. [RPCS.XIII.554]

MCKENNA, WILLIAM, a merchant in Belfast, petitioned the General Assembly of the Church of Scotland in 1643. [AGA.74] was admitted as a Free Merchant Stapler and Freen Commoner of Belfast in 1645. [TBB]

THE PEOPLE OF BELFAST, 1600-1799

MACKENZIE, ALEXANDER, of Saintfield, born 1634, died in Belfast during 1754, 'He left a widow who is but four years younger than himself.' [SM.16.155]

MACKENZIE, CHARLES, master of the Prince of Wales of Belfast bound for Pennsylvania, 1771-1772, [BNL]

MCKEOWN, ALEXANDER, born 1785, a labourer from Belfast, bound for New York aboard the Eagle of New York in 1803. [BL.Addl.ms.]

MCKERLY, JOHN, a tailor and a dealer in Belfast, was admitted as a Freeman of Belfast in 1752. [TBB]

MCKERN, BERNARD, lease of Peter's Hill, Belfast, 1780. [PRONI.D298.48]

MCKESNEY, ALEXANDER, a husbandman, was admitted as a Freeman of Belfast in 1639. [TBB]

MCKEWEN, THOMAS, master of the Martha of Belfast in 1747. [NRS.E504.4.1]

MCKIBBIN, EDWARD, a merchant, was admitted as a Freeman of Belfast in 1726. [TBB]

MCKIBBIN, HUGH, a tanner, born 1772, died 1817, husband of Sarah ,,,,,,, born 1782, died 1859. [New Burying Ground MI]

MCKIBBIN, JOHN, a cooper, was admitted as a Freeman of Belfast in 1725. [TBB]

MCKIBBIN, JOHN, born 1785, died 1833, husband of Margaret Warnock. [New Burying Ground MI]

MCKIE, THOMAS, a merchant burgess of Belfast, son and heir of Patrick McKie of Cairn, Wigtownshire, 1688, [NRS.S/H]

THE PEOPLE OF BELFAST, 1600-1799

MCKILLOP, CHARLES, from Belfast, emigrated aboard the Earl of Holderness, master William Blair, to Philadelphia in 1752. [Lancaster County Historical Society: Hanover Tax List]

MCKIMMIE, ALEXANDER, master of the Anna of Belfast 1696. [NRS.E72.19.23]

MCKINDLIS, ROBERT, master of the Providence of Belfast 1682. [NRS.E72.12.6]

MCKINLAY, DANIEL, master of the Robert of Belfast 1686. [NRS.E72.19.12]

MCKINLAY, ROBERT, master and merchant aboard the Providence of Belfast 1682. [NRS.E72.12.6]

MCKINNEY, ALEXANDER, from Belfast, emigrated on board the Angel Gabriel bound for Nevis and the West Indies in 1661. [PRONI.MIC19/1]

MCKITERICK, HUGH, a shoemaker, was admitted as a Freeman of Belfast in 1728. [TBB]

MCKITTRICK, SAMUEL, in Belfast, lease of a kiln in Goose Lane, Belfast, 1717. [PRONI.D509.42]

MCLAIN, DANIEL, a brickmaker of Strandmills, was admitted as a Freeman of Belfast in 1752. [TBB]

MACLAINE, WILLIAM, master of the William of Belfast 1683. [NRS.E72.3.12]

MACKLEN, JOHN, a mariner from Belfast, died aboard the Warrington in Guinea, probate 1692, PCC

MCLACHLAN, HENRY, a merchant in Belfast, testament, 1743, Comm. Edinburgh. [NRS]

MCLAUCHLAN, BERNARD, in Belfast, lease of McMinn's Entry, Belfast, in 1799. [PRONI.D298.94]

THE PEOPLE OF BELFAST, 1600-1799

MCLAUGHLIN, NEILL, a cooper, was admitted as a Freeman of Belfast in 1731. [TBB]

MCLEAN, WILLIAM, in Belfast, a lease, 1788. [PRONI.D199.13]

MCMACHEN, JOHN, master of the Janet of Belfast 1714. [NRS.E508.8.6]

MCMASTER, ROBERT, in Belfast, lease of a house on Hanover Quay, Belfast, in 1796. [PRONI.D298.90]

MCMATH, JOHN, a merchant in Belfast, was admitted as a burgess and guilds-brother of Ayr in 1697. [ABR]

MCMULLAN, HENRY, a butcher, was admitted as a Freeman of Belfast in 1783. [TBB]

MCMUNN, JOHN, lease of Rosemary Lane, Belfast, 1721. [PRONI.CR3.32.B.1.2]; a soap boiler, was admitted as a Freeman of Belfast in 1728. [TBB]

MCMURRAY, JOHN, a burgess, 1639, 1645. [TBB]

MCNAUGHTON, JOHN, of Petershill, a merchant in Belfast, a letter, 1716. [NRS.GD112.39.273.32]

MCNEIL, ARCHIBALD, in Belfast in 1669. [PRONI.T307A]

MCNEILE, ARCHIBALD, an apothecary in Belfast, witness to the will of Richard Hodgkinson, probate Dublin, 1720.

MCNEILL, ARCHIBALD, a surgeon in Belfast in 1748, nephew of Neil McNeill a surgeon apothecary there. [NRS.S/H]

MCNEILL, DANIEL, was admitted as a Free Stapler of Belfast in 1640. [TBB]

THE PEOPLE OF BELFAST, 1600-1799

MCNEILL, JOHN, master of the Pitt of Belfast bound for Maryland in1785, shipwrecked. [GM.IX.418.12],

MCNEILL, NEILL, an apothecary, who was admitted as a burgess of Belfast in 1702, [TBB.193]; a sasine, 1710. [NRS.RS9 (Argyll).4.96; 4.591; 5.173]; 1712, [Argyll Sheriff Court Book.7, 1722]; testament, 1733, [NRS.CC2.12.1.3]; a surgeon apothecary in Belfast died before 1748. [NRS.S/H]; a burgess 1703-1707. [BMF]

MACNELL, JOHN, master of the Resolution of Belfast 1681. [NRS.E72.20.5]

MCNIGHT, GEORGE, in Belfast in 1669. [PRONI.T307A]

MCQUARTERS, JOHN, from Belfast, died 1814 in Canada. [PRONI.D664/D351]

MCQUAY, JAMES, a chandler, formerly an apprentice to Arthur Thetford, was admitted as a Freeman of Belfast in 1729. [TBB]

MCQUERG, ALLEN, a merchant, was admitted as a Freeman of Belfast in 1730. [TBB]

MCQUOID, HUGH, a gunsmith, was admitted as a Freeman of Belfast in 1727. [TBB]

MCRAE, ALEXANDER, in Stranraer, formerly a merchant in Belfast, deeds, 1701, 1707. [NRS.RD4.89.589; RD4.101.595]

MCREENY, ALEXANDER, a cooper, was admitted as a Freeman of Belfast in 1728. [TBB]

MCRULLY, ROBERT, master of the Robert of Belfast 1685. [NRS.E72.12.10]

MCTEAR, DAVID, in Belfast, a deed, 1776. [PRONI.D199.8]; a lease in Belfast, 1800,

THE PEOPLE OF BELFAST, 1600-1799

[PRONI.D199/27]; a deed re Green Street, Belfast, in 1802. [PRONI.D199.25]

MCTIER, JOHN, a seaman from Belfast, to be released from Edinburgh or Canongate tolbooth in July 1689. [RPCS.XIII.554]

MCTEAR, MARGARET, in Belfast, lease in Mill Street, Belfast, in 1779. [PRONI.D509.601]

MCTEAR, SAMUEL, a lease in Goose Lane, Belfast, in 1754. [PRONI.D509.66]

MACUMBER, THOMAS, an adventurer who was granted land in the south-west-quarter of the barony of Belfast, 1643   [SPI.1642-1659: 354]

MCWATTERS, JAMES, a vintner, was admitted as a Freeman of Belfast in 1746. [TBB]

MCWHA, SAMUEL, a tailor, was admitted as a Freeman of Belfast in 1729. [TBB]

MCWILLIAM, JOHN, master of the Janet of Belfast trading with Stockholm, Sweden, and Flanders, 1716-1717. [NRS.E502.E508]

MAINE, JOHN, master of the Salmon of Belfast 1695. [NRS.E72.19.23]; master of the Friendship of Belfast trading with Charleston, South Carolina, in 1719. [TNA.CO5.508]

MAIN, ST JOHN, of the Falls, was admitted as a Freeman of Belfast in 1771. [TBB]

MAINFOD, WILLIAM, master of the James and Betty of Belfast in 1763. [NRS.E504.15.11]

MAINS, JOHN, a merchant in Belfast, was admitted as a burgess and guilds-brother of Ayr in 1736. [ABR]

THE PEOPLE OF BELFAST, 1600-1799

MAITLAND, JAMES, master of the Carolina of Belfast 1737. [TNA.CO5.509]; bound for South Carolina in 1744. [NRS.E504.26.1]

MAJOR, THOMAS, a tanner in Belfast, was admitted as a Freeman there in 1776. [TBB]

MALCOLMSON, SAMUEL, from Belfast, was naturalised in South Carolina in 1798. [NARA.M1183]

MANKIN, GEORGE, in Belfast, 1643. [TBB]

MANKIN, JOHN, a burgess of Bristol, 1639. [TBB]

MANKIN, WILLIAM, a silversmith, was admitted as a Freeman of Belfast in 1730. [TBB]

MANSFIELD, THOMAS, a burgess of Belfast, a letter 1754. [PRONI.D354.1007]

MANSON, DAVID, born 1727, a schoolmaster and freeman of Belfast in 1779, died 1792. [TBB]

MARK, ROBERT, in Belfast in 1645. [TBB]

MARSHALL, CHRISTOPHER, in Belfast in 1645. [TBB]

MARSHALL, THOMAS, a shoemaker, was admitted as a Free Commonr of Belfast in 1647. [TBB]

MARSHALL, TIMOTHY, was admitted as a Free Stapler of Belfast in 1644. [TBB]

MARSHALL, WILLIAM, merchant on the Elizabeth of Belfast 1695. [NRS.E72.19.23]

MARSTON, HENRY, in Belfast in 1645. [TBB]

MARTIN, GEORGE, was admitted as a Free Stapler of Belfast in 1635. [TBB]; a merchant in Belfast, died 1639. [PROI.RC9/1.37]

MARTIN, GEORGE, a Scot in Belfast, to be transported to the west of Ireland in 1653. [TBB]

MARTIN, GEORGE, a merchant burgess 1645-1678. [BMF]

MARTIN, HUGH, a yeoman, was admitted as a Freeman of Belfast in 1729. [TBB]

MARTIN, HUGH, a baker, was admitted as a Freeman of Belfast in 1746. [TBB]

MARTIN, JAMES, a mealman in Belfast, in Belfast, was admitted as a Free Commoner of Belfast in1646, [TBB]; in Belfast in 1669. [PRONI.T307A]

MARTIN, JAMES, of the Falls, was admitted as a Freeman of Belfast in 1771. [TBB]

MARTIN, JAMES, was admitted as a Freeman of Belfast in 1783. [TBB]

MARTIN, JOHN, a merchant, was admitted as a Free Stapler of Belfast in 1646. [TBB]

MARTIN, JOHN, master of the *Mary of Belfast* 1684. [NRS.E72.3.13]

MARTIN, JOHN, master of the *Mally of Belfast* 1772. [NRS.E504.8.5]

MARTIN, JOSIAS, was admitted as a Free Stapler of Belfast in 1654. [TBB]

MARTIN, ROBERT, master of the *Agnes of Belfast* 1672. [NRS.E72.10.3]

MARTIN, ROBERT, a merchant in Belfast, petitioned the Privy Council of Scotland in 1691. [RPCS.XVI.309]

THE PEOPLE OF BELFAST, 1600-1799

MARTIN, ROBERT, master of the Agnes of Belfast 1673. [NRS.E72.10.3]

MARTIN, SAMUEL, a farmer, was admitted as a Freeman of Belfast in 1728. [TBB]

MARTIN, THOMAS, born 1643, a merchant in Belfast, died 1685, husband of Florence Stewart, born 1655, died 1683. [Drumbeg MI, County Down]

MARTIN, WILLIAM, in Belfast, was apprenticed for five years aboard the James and Ellice of Belfast, in 1723. [PRONI.D354.385]

MASON, ROBERT, master of the Two Brothers of Belfast 1691. [NRS.E72.12.18]

MASTERTON, CHARLES, Presbyterian minister in Rosemary Street, Belfast, from 1723, died 1750. [F.VII.532]

MATTEAR, Dr JOHN, born 1727, died 1806. [New Burying Ground MI, Belfast]

MATHERS, MOSES, lease in Rosemary Lane, Belfast, 1755. [PRONI.D298.22]

MATTHEWS, ELIZA, born 1778, from Belfast, bound for Philadelphia aboard the snow George of Philadelphia in 1803. [BL.Addl.ms]

MATTHEWS, JAMES, in Belfast, lease of the Course in Belfast, 1770. [PRONI.D509.506]

MATTHEWS, JOHN, a merchant in Belfast, 1644; a tanner burgess of Belfast, 1645. [TBB]

MATTHEWS, JOHN, a merchant in Belfast, was admitted as a Freeman of Belfast in 1754. [TBB]

THE PEOPLE OF BELFAST, 1600-1799

MATTHEW, JOHN, a merchant, was admitted as a Freeman of Belfast in 1783. [TBB]

MATTHEWS, THOMAS, born 1776, a dealer from Belfast, bound for Philadelphia aboard the snow <u>George of Philadelphia</u> in 1803. [BL.Addl.ms]

MATHIE, ROBERT, master of the <u>Three ….of Belfast</u> in 1682, [NRS.E72.20.7] and of the <u>Janet of Belfast</u> in 1689. [NRS.E72.3.18]

MATTEAR, DAVID, a lease of Rosemary Lane, Belfast, 1787. [PRONI.CR3.32.B1.7]

MATTEAR, SAMUEL, jr., a merchant in Belfast, was admitted as a Freeman of Belfast in 1760. [TBB]

MAXWELL, ANDREW, a merchant in Belfast, a letter, 1672, in 1682, [TBB.152]; deeds, 1691, 1693. 1701, 1714. [NRS.RD2.71.1148; RD3.81.437; RD2.85.860 RD2.85.860]; 1694. [NRS.RH15.91.39/60]

MAXWELL, A. RAINEY, a witness in Belfast, 1737. [PRONI.D354.296]

MAXWELL, GEORGE, in Belfast, 1702, 1709. [NRS.CH1.5.6.187.190]

MAXWELL, JAMES, from Carrickfergus, was admitted as a Free Stapler and Free Commoner of Belfast in 1647. [TBB]

MAXWELL, JAMES, son of Arthur Maxwell (died 1720) and his wife Anne, a merchant in Belfast. [see Arthur Maxwell's will, probate 1721 Dublin]

MAXWELL, JAMES HAMILTON, a merchant in Belfast, co-owner of the <u>Priscilla of Belfast</u>, power of attorney, 1726. [PRONI.D354.615/616]

THE PEOPLE OF BELFAST, 1600-1799

MAXWELL, JOHN, a seaman from Belfast, to be released from Edinburgh or Canongate tollbooth, 1689. [RPCS.XIII.554]

MAXWELL, RAINEY, The Lodge, Belfast, a will, probate 1811. [NAI.T711]

MAXWELL, ROBERT, son of Andrew Maxwell a merchant in Belfast, a deed, 1714. [NRS.RD2.85.860]

MAXWELL, T., in Belfast, a letter, 1669. [PRONI.D695.147]

MAXWELL, WILLIAM, a merchant aboard the James of Belfast, a deed, 1691. [NRS.E72.19.21]

MAXWELL, WILLIAM, a chapman, was admitted as a Freeman of Belfast in 1728. [TBB]

MAYORS, ALEXANDER, a tailor, was admitted as a Freeman of Belfast in 1725. [TBB]

MEACH, MORICK, in Belfast, a bond, 1790. [PRONI.D491.42]

MEARS, JAMES, a factor in Belfast, 1726. [NRS.AC32.116-213; AC9.967]

MEEKE, FRANCIS, in Belfast in 1659. [C]; a burgess 1657-1665. [BMF]

MENTER, JOHN, born 1775, a labourer from Belfast, emigrated aboard the Eagle to New York in 1803. [BL.Add.Ms35392]

MERCER, BRIAN, co-owner of the Isaac of Belfast 1732. [PRONI.D354.417]

MERRYMAN, WILLIAM, a servant of William Wilson a merchant in Belfast, was admitted as a Freeman of Belfast in 1754. [TBB]

THE PEOPLE OF BELFAST, 1600-1799

MILLER, JAMES, was admitted as a Freeman of Belfast in 1639. [TBB]

MILLER, JOHN, from Antrim, the elder, a merchant, was admitted as a Merchant Stapler of Belfast in 1645. [TBB]

MILLER, JOHN, the younger, son of the above, was admitted as a Free Stapler of Belfast in 1644. [TBB]

MILLER, JOHN, a shoemaker, was admitted as a Freeman of Belfast in 1730. [TBB]

MILLER, Mrs SARAH, born 1772, died 1829. [Shankill MI, Belfast]

MILLIKEN, JAMES, a slater in Belfast, husband of Jane Sayers, born 1732, died 1798. [Shankill MI, Belfast]

MILLIKEN, THOMAS, born 1780, a merchant from Belfast, was naturalised in South Carolina in 1806. [NARA.M1183]

MILLIKEN, or GAW, wife of Thomas Milliken, an heir of Patrick Gaw in Belfast, 1792. [PRONI.D298.80]

MILLER, ROBERT, a carpenter in Belfast, was admitted as a Freeman of Belfast in 1760. [TBB]

MILLER, TIMOTHY, was admitted as a Free Stapler of Belfast in 1644. [TBB]

MILLER, WILLIAM, a shoemaker, was admitted as a Freeman of Belfast in 1728. [TBB]

MILLING, ARCHIBALD, master of the <u>Dove of Belfast</u>, 1691. [NRS.E72.12.18]

MILLS, ANDREW, a merchant in Belfast, a letter, 1756. [PRONI.D354.781]

THE PEOPLE OF BELFAST, 1600-1799

MILNE, TIMOTHY, in Belfast in 1645. [TBB]

MINIS, JOHN, of Long Lane, Belfast, was admitted as a Freeman of Belfast in 1747. [TBB]

MITCHELL, EDWARD, a merchant, was admitted as a Freeman of Belfast in 1726. [TBB]

MITCHELL, GEORGE, in Belfast, a lease in 1770. [PRONI.D491.31]

MITCHELL, GILBERT, in Belfast, 1669. [PRONI.T307A]

MITCHELL, JOHN, a gentleman, was admitted as a burgess of Belfast in 1642. [TBB]

MITCHELL, JOHN, a merchant aboard the Charles of Belfast bound for the West Indies in 1691. [NRS.E72.19.22]

MITCHELL, WILLIAM, in Belfast, a bill of exchange, 1727. [PRONI.D354.408]; a letter, 1734. [PRONI.D354.492]

MONEYPENNY, HUGH, son of the Town Sergeant, was admitted as a Freeman of Belfast in 1758. [TBB]

MONEYPENNY, WILLIAM, son of the Town Sergeant, was admitted as a Freeman of Belfast in 1758. [TBB]

MONTEITH, JOHN, a merchant in Belfast, was admitted as a burgess and guilds-brother of Ayr in 1688. [ABR]

MONTGOMERY, DAVID, in Belfast, 1669. [PRONI.T307A]

MONTGOMERY, HUGH, a merchant in Belfast, was admitted as a burgess and guilds-brother of Ayr in 1687. [ABR]

THE PEOPLE OF BELFAST, 1600-1799

MONTGOMERY, HUGH, in Belfast, a bill of exchange, 1732. [PRONI.D354.415]

MONTGOMERY, HUGH, a merchant in Belfast, was admitted as a Freeman there in 1776. [TBB]; a deed, 1792. [PRONI.D491.51]

MONTGOMERY, JAMES, a mariner, was admitted as a Freeman of Belfast in 1726. [TBB]

MONTGOMERY, JAMES, a land waiter in Belfast, a conveyance of premises in Skipper's Lane, Belfast, 1781; [PRONI.D238.53]; a lease of Orr's Entry in Belfast, in 1794. [PRONI.D298.88]

MONTGOMERY, JEREMIAH, born 1782, died 1842, husband of Mary ......, born 1784, died 1844. [Shankill MI, Belfast]

MONTGOMERY, JOHN, a lease of North Street, Belfast, 1731. [PRONI.D298.8]

MONTGOMERY, ROBERT, a merchant, was admitted as a Freeman of Belfast in 1727. [TBB]; a lease of North Street, Belfast, 1731. [PRONI.D298.8]; in Belfast, a lease, 1737. [PRONI.D389.16]

MONTGOMERY, THOMAS, in Belfast, 1669. [PRONI.T307A]; master of the John of Belfast 1672. [NRS.E72.10.3]

MONTGOMERY, WILLIAM, of Whitehouse, a merchant, was admitted as a Freeman of Belfast in 1729. [TBB]; a letter 1754. [PRONI.D354.1007]

MOOR, ALEXANDER, in Belfast, a letter, 1711; part owner of the Donegall of Belfast. [PRONI.D271.4]

MOORE, ANN, in Belfast, a conveyance of a tenement in Ann Street, Belfast, 1795. [PRONI.D199.20]

THE PEOPLE OF BELFAST, 1600-1799

MOORE, ARCHIBALD, a laborer, was admitted as a Freeman of Belfast in 1658. [TBB]

MOORE, EDWARD, was admitted as a Freeman of Belfast in 1640. [TBB]

MOORE, HENRY SHAW, was admitted as a Freeman of Belfast in 1796. [TBB]

MOORE, JAMES, son of John Moore in Belfast, heir to his grandmother Agnes Wilson, wife of Robert Lightbody a hatter in Ayr, 1788. [NRS.S/H]

MOORE, PATRICK, was admitted as a Freeman of Belfast in 1783. [TBB]

MOORE, RICHARD, a tanner, was admitted as a Freeman of Belfast in 1783. [TBB]

MOOR, WILLIAM, a merchant in Belfast, trading with France, 1720. [PRONI.D354.374]

MOORE, WILLIAM, was admitted as a Freeman of Belfast in 1783. [TBB]

MOORHEAD, ALEXANDER, was admitted as a Freeman of Belfast in 1727. [TBB]

MOORHEAD, JOSEPH, a carrier, was admitted as a Freeman of Belfast in 1731. [TBB]

MORLAND, JAMES, a butcher in Belfast, was admitted as a Freeman of Belfast in 1760. [TBB]

MORLEY, ROBERT, vicar of Belfast Corporation Church in 1622.

MORROW, JAMES, in Belfast, a lease of Lower Malone, Belfast, in 1770. [PRONI.D509.510]

THE PEOPLE OF BELFAST, 1600-1799

MORROW, SAMUEL, lease on Carrickfergus Street, Belfast in 1792. [PRONI.D298.82]

MORRISON, NATHANIEL, was admitted as a Freeman of Belfast in 1727. [TBB]

MORRISON, THOMAS, master of the Prince of Wales of Belfast bound for America in 1772. [BNL]

MORRISON, WILLIAM, master of the Prince of Wales of Belfast 1773. [BNL]

MORTON, ANDREW, a shoemaker, was admitted as a Freeman of Belfast in 1729. [TBB]

MUIR, ALEXANDER, a merchant in Belfast, nephew of John Craig a merchant burgess of Glasgow, was admitted as a burgess and guilds-brother of Glasgow in 1694. [GBR]

MUIR, JOHN, a merchant in Ralow, Belfast, son of Andrew Muir portioner of Over Auchintivybeit, Ayrshire, a sasine, 1627. [NRS.RS.4 (Ayrshire).122]

MUIR, JOHN, son of the late Andrew Muir in Belfast, apprenticed to a merchant in Edinburgh in 1640. [REA]

MUIR, JOHN, a merchant in Belfast, a deed, 1682. [NRS.RD2.58.21]; a merchant aboard the Ann of Belfast in 1682. [NRS.E72.19.5]

MULLIGAN, GILBERT, a gunsmith, was admitted as a Freeman of Belfast in 1726. [TBB]

MUNFORD, WILLIAM, a blacksmith, was admitted as a Freeman of Belfast in 1728. [TBB]

MUNN, ROBERT, master of the John of Belfast 1670. [NRS.E72.10.2]

THE PEOPLE OF BELFAST, 1600-1799

MUNRO, ALEXANDER, a merchant in Belfast, was admitted as a burgess of Glasgow, 1694. [PRONI.D271.3]

MUNRO, DANIEL, in Belfast, a lease in Fore Plantation, Belfast, 2804. [PRONI.D199.31]

MURCHIE, ARCHIBALD, master of the <u>Isabel of Belfast</u> 1667. [NRS.E72.9.3]

MURDOCH, JAMES, a cooper, was admitted as a Freeman of Belfast in 1727. [TBB]

MURDOCH, JOSEPH, in Belfast, a deed, 1794. [PRONI.D470.14]

MURRAY, DANIEL, master of the <u>James and Robert of Belfast</u> 1696. [NRS.E72.19.23]

MURRAY, GEORGE, a weaver in Belfast, was admitted as a Freeman of Belfast in 1761. [TBB]

MURRAY, HENRY, a weaver, was admitted as a Free Commoner of Belfast in 1650. [TBB]

MURRAY, JOHN, in Belfast, 1669. [PRONI.T307A]

MURRAY, PATRICK, a lease in Peter's Hill, Belfast 1791. [PRONI.D298.77]

MURRAY, ROBERT, master of the <u>George of Belfast</u> 1689, [NRS.E72.19.15]; master of the <u>Jane of Belfast</u> bound for Virginia in 1692, the ship was captured off Newfoundland by a French privateer. [TNA.HCA.Exams,80];master of the <u>Loyalty of Belfast</u> trading with Virginia in1699. [TNA.CO5.1441]

MURRAY, ROBERT, a tailor in Dublin, was admitted as a Freeman of Belfast in 1730. [TBB]

THE PEOPLE OF BELFAST, 1600-1799

MUSSENDEN, DANIEL, a merchant in Belfast from 1720 until his death in 1763. [PRONI.D354]; trustee of James Smith a brewer in Belfast, 1720; a deed, 1745, [PRONI.D354.307]; owner of the Marlborough of Belfast trading with Spain, 1712. [PRONI.D354.359]; co-owner of the Hanover of Belfast a charter party re voyage to America, 1717, [PRONI.D354.363]; co-owner of the Friendship of Belfast bound for Charleston, South Carolina, in 1718, a charter party, [PRONI.D354.370]; in 1731, [NRS.GD10.483]; trading with Spain and Gibraltar, 1724, [PRONI.D354.493]; a letter, 1745, [PRONI.D354.307]; a banker in Belfast, 1752. [TBB][UJA.II.1.161]; a burgess of Belfast, a letter 1754. [PRONI.D354.1007]; a merchant and banker in Belfast from 1720 until his death in 1763.[PRONI.D354]

MUSSENDEN, WILLIAM, born 1712, son of Daniel Mussenden, a merchant in Belfast who died 1794. [PRONI.D304]

MUSSENDEN, ADAIR AND BATESON, bankers in Belfast, 1753 to 1763. [PRONI]

NAIRN, Dr, in Belfast in 1645. [TBB]

NEEVANS, ROBERT, a burgess of Belfast in 1639. [TBB]

NEIL, JAMES, of Kilead, was admitted as a Freeman of Belfast in 1773. [TBB]

NEILL, PATRICK, a printer in Belfast, 1694, [TBB]; a merchant in Belfast, a deed, 1697. [NRS.RD2.80/2.672]

NEILL, ROBERT, apprentice to James Watt, was admitted as a Freeman of Belfast in 1730. [TBB]

NEILL, WILLIAM, a mariner from Belfast, was naturalised in South Carolina in 1797. [NARA.M1183]

THE PEOPLE OF BELFAST, 1600-1799

NEILSON, JOHN, a lease of Rosemary Lane, Belfast, 1787. [PRONI.CR3.32.B1.7]

NEILSON, ROBERT, a butcher in Belfast, was admitted as a Freeman of Belfast in 1774. [TBB]

NEILSON, THOMAS, a butcher, was admitted as a Freeman of Belfast in 1767. [TBB]

NETHERFIELD, CHRISTOPHER, master of the Beggar's Bennison of Belfast in 1770. [NRS.E504.15.18]

NEVIN, ROBERT, a merchant, was admitted as a Freeman of Belfast in 1658. [TBB.249]

NEWBY, PETER, was admitted as a Freeman of Belfast in 1742. [TBB]

NEWELL, JANE, in Belfast, a bond, 1791. [PRONI.D491.50]

NEWMAN, JOHN, a peruke-maker, was admitted as a Freeman of Belfast in 1728. [TBB]

NICHOLSON, SOPHIA, in Belfast, lease of a house on Hanover Quay, Belfast, in 1796. [PRONI.D298.90]

NOCHER, JAMES, a coal porter in Belfast, was admitted as a Freeman of Belfast in 1737. [TBB]

NORRIS, THOMAS, born 1748, a farmer from Belfast, bound for New York on the Eagle, master Charles Thompson, in 1804. [BL.Addl. ms]

NORVELL, JOHN, a merchant in Glasgow, was admitted as a Freeman of Belfast in 1656. [TBB249]

NUTT, WILLIAM, a hatter, was admitted as a Freeman of Belfast in 1730. [TBB]

THE PEOPLE OF BELFAST, 1600-1799

O'DIDLE, ELIAS, of the Falls of Belfast, was admitted as a Freeman of Belfast in 1737. [TBB]

OGANS, SLOAN, a butcher in Belfast, was admitted as a Freeman of Belfast in 1760. [TBB]

O'GILLAN, DANIEL, was admitted as a Freeman of Belfast in 1731. [TBB]

O'HADDEN, JOHN, a shoemaker in Belfast, was admitted as a Freeman of Belfast in 1638. [TBB]

O'HANLAN, BRYAN, a cutler, was admitted as a Freeman of Belfast in 1730. [TBB]

O'HAMILL, BRYAN, was admitted as a Freeman of Belfast in 1728. [TBB]

O'HARTAN, EDMOND, a carpenter, was admitted as a Freeman of Belfast in 1635. [TBB]

O'KENNAN, DERMOTT, a burgess of Belfast in 1639. [TBB]

O'KENNAN, MICHAEL, of Skigin Earle, was admitted as a Freeman of Belfast in 1752. [TBB]

O'KENNAN, OWEN, servant to Isaac McCartney, was admitted as a Freeman of Belfast in 1730. [TBB]

O'MALLEN, DANIEL, died 1730. [Shankill MI, Belfast]

ORR, ALEXANDER, a merchant, was admitted as a Freeman of Belfast in 1726. [TBB]

ORR, ALEXANDER, born 1779 in Belfast, naturalised in New York, 1804.[TBB]

ORR, GILBERT, a merchant, was admitted as a Freeman of Belfast in 1747. [TBB]

THE PEOPLE OF BELFAST, 1600-1799

ORR, JOHN, a merchant, was admitted as a Free Commoner of Belfast in 1647. [TBB]

ORR, ROBERT, of Newtown, a wheelwright, was admitted as a Freeman of Belfast in 1752. [TBB]

OSBURNE, JANET, a refugee from Belfast, in Ayr 1642. [NRS.CH2.751.2/383]

OSBURN, JOHN, a baker, was admitted as a Freeman of Belfast in 1725. [TBB]

OSEY, CLEMENT, registrar of butchers in Belfast, 1622. [TBB]

PARK, JAMES, a merchant in Belfast, 1726, trustee of the will of James Smith, probate 1726, Dublin

PARK, JOHN, in Belfast, a lease in 1770. [PRONI.D509.512]

PARRY, NICHOLAS, an adventurer who was granted land in the north-west-quarter of the barony of Belfast, 1643   [SPI.1642-1659: 354]

PARTRIDGE, ROBERT, a burgess of Belfast, 1639. [TBB]

PARTRIDGE, WILLIAM, a burgess of Belfast, 1639. [TBB]

PARTIDGE, the widow, an innkeeper in Belfast, 1654. [TBB]

PATTEN, NEAL, a baker, was admitted as a Freeman of Belfast in 1729. [TBB]

PATTERSON, ADAM, servant of William Montgomery a merchant in Belfast, was admitted as a burgess and guilds-brother of Ayr, 1717. [ABR]

PATTERSON, ALEXANDER, was admitted as a Freeman of Belfast in 1771. [TBB]

THE PEOPLE OF BELFAST, 1600-1799

PATERSON, GEORGE, a tailor, was admitted as a Freeman of Belfast in 1726. [TBB]

PATTERSON, JAMES, a merchant in Belfast, was admitted as a Freeman of Belfast in 1772. [TBB]; executor of Mary McWalters in Belfast, 1781. [PRONI.D199.10]

PATERSON, JOHN, a shipmaster from Irvine, Ayrshire, was admitted as a Freeman of Belfast in 1737. [TBB]

PATTERSON, JOHN, servant to the Sovereign, was admitted as a Freeman of Belfast in 1766. [TBB]

PAYNE, WILLIAM, master of the Nancy of Belfast 1773. [NRS.E504.15.22]

PEART, JOHN, a butcher, was admitted as a Freeman of Belfast in 1728. [TBB]

PEASELY, Captain GEORGE, was admitted as a Freeman of Belfast in 1640. [TBB]

PENTLAND, JOHN, a merchant, was admitted as a Free Stapler of Belfast in 1643. [TBB]

PETYGREW, HUGH, a farmer, was admitted as a Freeman of Belfast in 1728. [TBB]

PETTYCREW, JOHN, a merchant, was admitted as a Freeman of Belfast in 1731. [TBB]

PICKEN, JAMES, a staymaker, was admitted as a Freeman of Belfast in 1752. [TBB]

PINKERTON, JAMES, a baker in Belfast, former apprentice to his father David Pinkerton, was admitted as a Freeman of Belfast in 1748. [TBB]

THE PEOPLE OF BELFAST, 1600-1799

PITCHER, WILLIAM, an adventurer who was granted land in the north-west-quarter of the barony of Belfast, 1643   [SPI.1642-1659: 354]

PITT, JOHN, senior, a burgess of Belfast in 1646. [TBB]

PLOMER, MATHEW, was admitted as a Freeman of Belfast in 1725. [TBB]

POAG, CHARLES, master of the <u>Charming Polly of Belfast</u> 1771. [NRS.E504.8.5]

POLEWHEELE, PETER, a gentleman in Belfast in 1659. [C]

POLLOCK, MARTHA, in Belfast, a lease, 1770. [PRONI.D509.429]

POLLOCK, WILLIAM, a shoemaker, was admitted as a Freeman of Belfast in 1746. [TBB]

PORTER, THOMAS, master of the <u>Nightingale of Belfast</u> 1686. [NRS.E72.19.12]

PORTIS, GEORGE, a burgess of Belfast 1707, [BMF]; a letter 1754. [PRONI.D354.1007]; a letter, 1770. [PRONI.D572.2.42]

POSTELY, THOMAS, town sergeant of Belfast, 1640. [TBB]

POSTLEY, THOMAS, jr., was admitted as a Freeman of Belfast in 1640. [TBB]

POTTER, JAMES, a shop-keeper, was admitted as a Freeman of Belfast in 1725. [TBB]

POTTINGER, Captain EDWARD, master of the <u>Insiquin of Belfast</u> in the 1660s/1670s, and of the <u>Donegall</u> in the 1680s; a merchant in Belfast was admitted as a burgess and guilds-brother of Ayr in 1689. [ABR]; in 1688 he

THE PEOPLE OF BELFAST, 1600-1799

raised a company of soldiers to defend Coleraine, later he was appointed Captain of HM Yacht Fanfan and fought at the Siege of Carrickfergus, subsequently he was Captain of HMS Dartmouth which was wrecked in a storm when he drowned in 1690, leaving a wife and children. He was brother to Thomas Pottinger, a sovereign of Belfast. [RPCS.XVI.4]

POTTINGER, THOMAS, former sovereign of Belfast, petitioned the Privy Council of Scotland in 1691. [RPCS.XVI.4]

POTTS, JOHN, a bookseller, was admitted as a Freeman of Belfast in 1731. [TBB]; a member of the Third Presbyterian Meeting House, Belfast, 1749. [PRONI.D298.16]

POTTS, PETER, was admitted as a Free Commoner and Sergeant of Belfast in 1653. [TBB]

PRINCE, MAGNUS, in Belfast, 1738. [NRS.AC20.2.6]

PRINGLE, WILLIAM, master of the barque Nightingale of Belfast 1681, 1686, 1689. [NRS.E72.3.5; E72.3.6/19]

PUMPHY, JOHN, born 1774, a farmer from Belfast, bound for Philadelphia aboard the snow George of Philadelphia in 1803. [BL.Addl.ms]

QUINN, THOMAS, in Belfast in 1645. [TBB]

RAA, EDWARD, a laborer, was admitted as a Freeman of Belfast in 1730. [TBB]

RADCLIFFE, FRANCIS, a burgess of Belfast in 1639. [TBB]

RAE, HUGH, a merchant in Belfast, a deed, 1702. [NRS.RD2.86.1.488]

THE PEOPLE OF BELFAST, 1600-1799

RAINEY, WILLIAM, a merchant in Belfast, 1722. [NRS.AC9.849]

RAMAGE, CHARLES, a carrier in Belfast, was admitted as a Freeman of Belfast in 1772. [TBB]

RAMSAY, JOHN, in the Liberties of Belfast, 1669. [PRONI.T307A]

RAMSAY, THOMAS, in Belfast, 1669. [PRONI.T307A]

RAMSAY, THOMAS, in Belfast, a lease in Millfield, Belfast, 1790. [PRONI.D296.74]

RAMSAY, WILLIAM, merchant aboard the <u>Providence of Belfast</u>, 1689. [NRS.E72.3.20]

RAMSAY, WILLIAM, a lease in Carrickfergus Street, Belfast, 1778. [PRONI.D298.46]

RANEY, WILLIAM, in Belfast, owner of the <u>Jane</u>, 1693. [TNA.HCA.Exams.81:21.1.1693]

RANKIN, CHARLES, a partner in the bank Cunningham, Rankin, Brown and Campbell in Belfast in 1784, later a partner in Hamilton and Rankin a bank in Belfast in 1798. [UJA.II.1.162]

RANKIN, JAMES, master of the <u>Janet of Belfast</u> 1691. [NRS.E72.19.21/22]

RANKIN, NATHANIEL, master of the <u>Sara of Belfast</u> 1721. [NRS.AC9.757]

RATCLIFF, FRANK, burgess of Belfast in 1646. [TBB]

RATELOCKE, JOHN W., a burgess of Belfast in 1639.[TBB]

RATLIFF, JOHN, a linen merchant, was admitted as a Freeman of Belfast in 1728. [TBB]

THE PEOPLE OF BELFAST, 1600-1799

RAWDEN, GEORGE, a burgess of Belfast in 1646. [TBB]

READ, JAMES, a tailor, was admitted as a Free Commoner of Belfast in 1650. [TBB]

REDMOND. Major DANIEL, Member of Parliament for Belfast, 1654. [TBB]

REID, ALEXANDER, a merchant, was admitted as a Free Commoner of Belfast in 1651. [TBB]

REID, DANIEL, a mariner probably from Belfast, who died aboard HMS Sheerness, probate 1698, PCC

REID, JAMES, a seaman from Belfast, to be released from Edinburgh or Canongate tolbooths in 1689. [RPCS.XIII.554]

REID,......, in the barony of Belfast, 1659. [C]

REILLY, HUGH, clerk to John Arnold an attorney, was admitted as a Freeman of Belfast in 1730. [TBB]

REYNELLS, EDWARD, was admitted as a Free Commoner of Belfast in 1652, [TBB]; a gentleman burgess 1660-1682. [BMF]

RICHARD, JAMES, a carder in Belfast, a sasine, 1628. [NRS.RS (Ayrshire).4.273]

RICHARD, WILLIAM, a tanner in Belfast, a sasine, 1628. [NRS.RS (Ayrshire).4.274]

RICHARDSON, NEHEMIUS, a candlemaker, was admitted as a Merchant Stapler and Free Commoner of Belfast in 1645. [TBB]

RICHARDSON, WILLIAM, was admitted as a Freeman of Belfast in 1754. [TBB]

RICHEY, DAVID, in Belfast in 1645. [TBB]

THE PEOPLE OF BELFAST, 1600-1799

RICHIE, WILLIAM, a merchant burgess of Ayr, was admitted as a Free Stapler of Belfast in 1647. [TBB]

RIDDEN, GEORGE, master of the *Mally of Belfast* in 1771. [NRS.E504.4.5]

RIDGBY, JOHN, was admitted as a Freeman of Belfast in 1647. [TBB]; a gentleman in Belfast in 1659. [C]; a tanner burgess 1655-1669. [BMF]

RIGGS, JOHN, a carman, was admitted as a Freeman of Belfast in 1730. [TBB]

RITCHEY, WILLIAM, a shoemaker, was admitted as a Freeman of Belfast in 1730. [TBB]

RITCHIE, WILLIAM, of the Belfast shipyard, 1791. [TBB]

ROAN, ARCHIBALD, was admitted as a Free Commoner of Belfast in 1654. [TBB]

ROBERTS, GEORGE, of the Falls, was admitted as a Freeman of Belfast in 1771. [TBB]

ROBERTS, JEREMIAH, a cutler and instrument maker in Belfast, was admitted as a burgess and freeman of Ayr in 1729. [ABR]

ROBERTSON, GEORGE, merchant on the *James of Belfast* 1695. [NRS.E72.19.23]

ROBINSON, BENJAMIN, a yeoman in Belfast, witness to the will of John Buchanan, probate, 1784, Dublin.

ROBINSON, JAMES, married Peggy McAdam, in Belfast in 1766. [FDJ.4084]

ROBINSON, JANE, born 1778, a spinstress from Belfast, bound for New York on the *Eagle*, master Charles Thompson, in 1804. [BL.Addl.ms]

THE PEOPLE OF BELFAST, 1600-1799

ROBINSON, JOHN, a merchant in Belfast, was admitted as a Freeman of Belfast in 1774. [TBB]

ROBISON, FRANCIS, was admitted as a Freeman of Belfast in 1644. [TBB]

ROBYNS, ROGER, town clerk of Belfast in 1640. [TBB]

RODDY, ANN, born 1747, died 1833, mother of Robert Roddy, born 1775, died 1803. [Shankill MI, Belfast]

RODGER, JOHN, a merchant, was admitted as a Free Commoner and Staple Merchant of Belfast in 1653. [TBB]

RODGER, JOHN, a yarn merchant, was admitted as a Freeman of Belfast in 1730. [TBB]

ROGERS, JOHN, a butcher, was admitted as a Freeman of Belfast in 1768. [TBB]

ROGERS, ROBERT, master of the Hopewell of Belfast trading with Charleston, South Carolina, and Barbados in 1735. [TNA.CO5.509]

ROGERS, WILLIAM, was admitted as a Freeman of Belfast in 1728. [TBB]

ROMINGE, WILLIAM, in Belfast in 1645. [TBB]

ROPER, GEORGE, master of the Hanover of Belfast bound for Bremen and Rotterdam, 1737. [PRONI.D354.512/515]

ROPER, WILLIAM, master of the James and Ellice of Belfast bound for France, charter party 1720. [PRONI.D354.374]

RORKE, THOMAS, a gentleman, was admitted as a Freeman of Belfast in 1639. [TBB]

THE PEOPLE OF BELFAST, 1600-1799

ROSS, ANDREW, master of the Katherine of Belfast 1715. [NRS.E72.E508.9.6]

ROSS, GEORGE, of Castle Lyons, a gentleman, was admitted as a Freeman of Belfast in 1730. [TBB]

ROSS, GILBERT, in Belfast, 1669. [PRONI.T307A]

ROSS, JAMES, in Belfast, 1669. [PRONI.T307A]

ROSS, JAMES, in Portlivoe, was admitted as a Freeman of Belfast in 1737. [TBB]; in Belfast, a witness in 1737, [PRONI.D354.296]; a deed, 1748. [PRONI.D552.B.1.1.1193]; a merchant in Belfast in 1758. [PRONI.D354.1010]; a will, 1796. [PRONI.D282.32]

ROSS, JOHN, in Belfast, a lease, 1737. [PRONI.D298.10]

ROYD, WILLIAM, was admitted as a Freeman of Belfast in 1733. [TBB]

ROYE, JOHN, a burgess of Belfast in 1639. [TBB]

RUSSELL, GEORGE, in Belfast, a lease, 1770. [PRONI.D509.515]

RUSSELL, JAMES, was admitted as a Freeman of Belfast in 1638. [TBB]

RUSSELL, JAMES, in Hollywood, was admitted as a Freeman of Belfast in 1727. [TBB]

RUSSELL, JOHN, master of the Fidelity of Belfast in 1743, of the Samuel of Belfast trading with Barbados in 1744, of the John and Matty of Belfast in 1775. [NRS.E504.34.1; 15.1; 8.5]

RUSSELL, TIMOTHY, in Hollywood, was admitted as a Freeman of Belfast in 1727. [TBB]

THE PEOPLE OF BELFAST, 1600-1799

SALTERS, WILLIAM, of the Falls, was admitted as a Freeman of Belfast in 1771. [TBB]

SALTUS, RICHARD, a butcher, was admitted as a Free Commoner of Belfast in 1655. [TBB]

SAMBROOKE, WILLIAM, was admitted as a Freeman of Belfast in 1643. [TBB]

SANDALL, JOHN, in Belfast, 16... [NRS.GD406.1.10667]

SANDERSON, JOHN, was admitted as a Freeman of Belfast in 1644. [TBB]

SANDS, HENRY, a gentleman, was admitted as a Free Stapler of Belfast in 1637. [TBB]

SANDS, WILLIAM, in Belfast in 1645. [TBB]

SARGASON, PATRICK, a yeoman in Belfast, witness to the will of John Buchanan, probate, 1784, Dublin.

SATTERTHWAITE, JOHN, a merchant, was admitted as a Freeman of Belfast in 1730. [TBB]

SAUNDERS, MARGARETSON, a merchant in Belfast, 1754. [PRONI.D270.5]; Sovereign there, a letter, 1754. [PRONI.D354.1007]

SAUNDERS, Lieutenant THOMAS, was admitted as a Freeman of Belfast in 1753. [TBB]

SAUNDERS, THOMAS, a merchant in Belfast, was admitted as a Freeman of Belfast in 1754. [TBB]

SAURIN, Reverend JAMES, vicar of Belfast Corporation Church in 1747, was admitted as a Freeman of Belfast in 1753, [TBB]; a lease of Upper Malone in Belfast also of Mount Collier there, in 1770. [PRONI.D509.520/521]; died 1772. [TBB]

THE PEOPLE OF BELFAST, 1600-1799

SAVAGE, H., at Mount Pottinger, Belfast, a letter 1780. [PRONI.D618.5]

SAVAGE, PATRICK, a mariner of Belfast, who died at sea aboard the ship *Edgar*, probate 1695, PCC

SAYERS, WILLIAM, a publican and linen manufacturer in Belfast, was admitted as a Freeman of Belfast in 1773. [TBB]

SAYERS, WILLIAM, of Shankill, born 1737, died 1802. [Shankill MI, Belfast]

SCOTT, DAVID, in Belfast, 1669. [PRONI.T307A]

SCOTT, HUGH, in Belfast, 1669. [PRONI.T307A]

SCOTT, JAMES, in Belfast, 1669. [PRONI.T307A]

SCOTT, JAMES, master of the *Margaret of Belfast* 1673. [NRS.E72.3.3]

SCOTT, JOHN, master of the *Content of Belfast* in 1676, also trading with France in 1681, [RPCS.II.582] [SPDom.1681.228/280]; in 1684. [NRS.E72.3.13]

SCOTT, MATTHEW, master of the *Concord of Belfast* in 1686, master of the *Elizabeth of Belfast* 1689, and of the *Prosperity of Belfast* 1691. [NRS.E72.12.13; E72.19.14/21]; master of the *Upton of Belfast* trading with Catelonia in 1705. [SPDom42.119.193; SPDom.iv.171]

SCOTT, ROBERT, a former apprentice in Belfast, a tailor, was admitted as a Freeman of Belfast in 1748. [TBB]

SCOTT, SAMUEL, a maltster in Belfast, was admitted as a Freeman of Belfast in 1761. [TBB]

THE PEOPLE OF BELFAST, 1600-1799

SCOTT, THOMAS, owner of the Content of Belfast 1676. [RPCS.III.583]

SCOTT, WALTER, in Belfast, 1669. [PRONI.T307A]

SCOTT, WILLIAM, in Belfast, owner of the Jane of Belfast, trading with Virginia in 1684. [TNA.HCA.Exams.81:21.1.1693]

SCOTT, WILLIAM, master of the Betty Gregg of Belfast in 1772. [NRS.E504.8.5]; trading between Belfast, Madeira, and Maryland in 1773-1774. [BNL]

SCOTT, WILLIAM, born 1702, died 1777, husband of Anne ....., born 1707, died 1779. [Shankill MI, Belfast]

SEED, FRANCIS, a merchant in Belfast, a letter, 1756. [PRONI.D354.781]; a lease in Weigh-house Lane, Belfast, 1770. [PRONI.D243.6]

SEEDS, WILLIAM, born 1679, a merchant in Belfast, died 1746. [Derriaghy MI, County Antrim]; was admitted as a Freeman of Belfast in 1729. [TBB]

SEEDS, WILLIAM, was admitted as a Freeman of Belfast in 1767. [TBB]

SEMPLE, JOHN, a meal-monger, was admitted as a Freeman of Belfast in 1729. [TBB]

SHANAHAN, Mrs ELIZABETH, born 1763, died 1790, wife of Daniel Shanahan of Belfast. [Shankill MI, Belfast]

SHANNAN, JOHN, a tailor, was admitted as a Freeman of Belfast in 1728. [TBB]

SHANNAN, JOHN, a tailor, was admitted as a Freeman of Belfast in 1730. [TBB]

SHANNAN, WILLIAM, a merchant, was admitted as a Freeman of Belfast in 1731. [TBB]

THE PEOPLE OF BELFAST, 1600-1799

SHARP, JOHN, a merchant, was admitted as a Freeman of Belfast in 1726. [TBB]

SHARSON, RICHARD, born 1785, Scripture Reader in Christ Church, died 1865. [Shankill MI]

SHAW, ANTHONY, graduated MA from Edinburgh University in 1639, a minister in Belfast from 1646 to 1649. [F.3.120; F.7.532]

SHAW, JOHN, a coach, wheel, and carriage maker, was admitted as a Freeman of Belfast in 1730. [TBB]

SHAW, JOHN, a tanner, was admitted as a Freeman of Belfast in 1746. [TBB]

SHAW, WILLIAM, a tanner, was admitted as a Freeman of Belfast in 1746. [TBB]

SHAW, WILLIAM, born 1775, died 1840. [Shankill MI]

SHEARER, JAMES, master of the doggar Matthew of Belfast was admitted as a burgess and guilds-brother of Ayr in 1725. [ABR]; master of the Batchelor of Belfast bound for Stockholm, Sweden, 1729. [NRS.E502]

SHEARER, THOMAS, a seaman from Belfast, to be released from Edinburgh or Canongate tolbooth in 1689. [RPCS.XIII.554]

SHEARER, ROBERT, master of the William of Belfast 1689. [NRS.E72.19.14]

SHIELDS, THOMAS, a cooper, was admitted as a Freeman of Belfast in 1746. [TBB]

SHIPBOY, ELIZABETH and JAMES, 18 High Street, Belfast, 1791. [PRONI.D530.7]

SHIPBOY, JAMES, in Belfast, a letter, 1793. [PRONI.D530.22]

THE PEOPLE OF BELFAST, 1600-1799

SIBBALD, WILLIAM, in Belfast, a deed, 1692. [PRONI.D509.31]

SIMM, ARTHUR, a tanner in Belfast, was admitted as a Freeman of Belfast in 1774. [TBB]

SIMM, ROBERT, a tanner in Belfast, was admitted as a Freeman of Belfast in 1774. [TBB]

SIM, WILLIAM, a saddler, was admitted as a Free Commoner of Belfast in 1647. [TBB]

SIMMS, ANN, a deed re Rosemary Lane, Belfast, in 1804. [PRONI.CR3.32B.21.2]

SIMMS, JANE, a deed re Rosemary Lane, Belfast, in 1804. [PRONI.CR3.32B.21.2]

SIMMS, ROBERT, a lease of Rosemary Lane, Belfast, 1787. [PRONI.CR3.32.B1.7]; similar in 1804. [PRONI.CR3.32.B.2.2]

SIMSON, FRANCIS, probably from Belfast, a surgeon aboard HMS Martha at Bengal, probate 1696 PCC

SIMPSON, JOHN, from Belfast, surgeon aboard the Edward and Francis of London probate 1694, PCC

SIMPSON, JOSEPH, a merchant, was admitted as a Freeman of Belfast in 1728. [TBB]; in Belfast, a lease, 1737. [PRONI.D298.10]

SIMPSON, WILLIAM, in Belfast, a lease, 1737. [PRONI.D298.10]

SINCLAIR, ALEXANDER, in Belfast in 1645. [TBB]; a merchant, was admitted as a Free Commoner of Belfast in 1647. [TBB]; in Belfast, 1669. [PRONI.T307A]

SINCLAIR, JAMES, a tailor, son of Robert Sinclair, was admitted as a Freeman of Belfast in 1730. [TBB]

THE PEOPLE OF BELFAST, 1600-1799

SINCLAIR, JOHN, born 1662, a sailor from Belfast, a witness in 1693. [TNA.HCA.Exams:81; 21.1.1693]

SINCLAIR, JOHN, a linen draper in Belfast, was admitted as a Freeman of Belfast in 1755. [TBB]

SINCLAIR, ROBERT, merchant on the Lewis of Belfast 1695. [NRS.E72.19.23]

SINCLAIR, THOMAS, a linen draper in Belfast, was admitted as a Freeman of Belfast in 1755. [TBB]

SINCLAIR, WILLIAM, born 1679, a merchant in Belfast, died 1759, husband of [1] Jane Gregg, and [2] Jane Scott [1685-1760]. [Belfast MI]

SLOAN, JOHN, former apprentice to Timothy Shields a baker, was admitted as a Freeman of Belfast in 1728. [TBB]

SMALLSHAW, THOMAS, a blockmaker, was admitted as a Freeman of Belfast in 1730. [TBB]

SMITH, ANDREW, son of Samuel Smith in Belfast, 1726. [NRS.GD113.4.109.384]; a merchant, was admitted as a Freeman of Belfast in 1727. [TBB]; a burgess of Belfast, a letter 1754. [PRONI.D354.1007]

SMITH, DAVID, master of the Speedwell of Belfast 1689. [NRS.E72.3.18]; master of the William and David of Belfast 1690. [NRS.E72.19.16]

SMITH, DAVID, a burgess of Belfast, at the Synod of Ulster at Antrim in 1697. [GSU.15]; a merchant burgess 1690-1705. [BMF]

SMITH, EDWARD, was admitted as a Freeman of Belfast in 1647. [TBB]

SMITH, HENRY, merchant on the Anna of Belfast 1696. [NRS.E72.12.6]

THE PEOPLE OF BELFAST, 1600-1799

SMITH, JAMES, a weaver, was admitted as a Freeman of Belfast in 1725. [TBB]

SMITH, JAMES, a merchant, was admitted as a Freeman of Belfast in 1729. [TBB]

SMITH, JAMES, a burgess of Belfast, 1639. [TBB]; in Belfast, 1651. [TBB]

SMITH, JAMES, a brewer in North Street, Belfast, spouse of Hanna Smith, father of James, Sarah, Elizabeth and Mary, probate 1726, Dublin

SMITH, JANET, in Belfast, a letter, 1804. [NRS.CH12.30.83]

SMITH, JOHN, a merchant from Belfast based in Ayr, 1690. [NRS.E72.3.20/21]

SMITH, JOHN, a merchant, was admitted as a Freeman of Belfast in 1727. [TBB]

SMITH, JOHN, a peruke-maker, was admitted as a Freeman of Belfast in 1730. [TBB]

SMITH, JOHN, in Belfast, a lease in 1770. [PRONI.D509.431]

SMYTH, JOHN, a merchant in Belfast, witness to the will of Thomas McIlwain, 1777.

SMITH, NATHAN, a merchant, was admitted as a Freeman of Belfast in 1728. [TBB]

SMITH, PATRICK, son of Samuel Smith, a merchant in Belfast, was admitted as a burgess of Glasgow in 1707. [GBR]

SMITH, PATRICK, in Belfast, a bill of exchange, 1733. [PRONI.D354.420A]

THE PEOPLE OF BELFAST, 1600-1799

SMITH, ROBERT, a merchant, was admitted as a Freeman of Belfast in 1728. [TBB]

SMITH, SAMUEL, in Belfast, 1726, [NRS.GD113.4.109.384]; a bill of exchange, 1733. [PRONI.D54.420A]; a witness in Belfast, 1737. [PRONI.D354.296]

SMITH, SAMUEL, a member of the Third Presbyterian Meeting House, Belfast, 1749. [PRONI.D298.16]; a merchant in Belfast and an emigration agent in 1753, [BNL:29.5.1753]

SMITH, SARAH, in Belfast, a lease of Shankill, Belfast, in 1770. [PRONI.D509.524]

SMITH, THOMAS, a blacksmith, was admitted as a Free Commoner of Belfast in 1647. [TBB]

SMITH, WILLIAM, a seaman aboard the Merchants Adventure of Belfast 1682. [NRS.E72.19.5]

SMITH, WILLIAM, an alderman of Belfast, 1702. [ECA.Moses.163/6297]

SMITH, ..., a merchant in Belfast, was admitted as a burgess of Edinburgh in 1704. [REB]

SMYLIE, JAMES, a stone-cutter in Belfast, father of Joseph Smylie, born 1807, died 1817. [Shankill MI, Belfast]

SMYLIE, JOHN, a co-partner of the Belfast Glass House Company, deed of partnership, 1791. [PRONI.]

SNELL, Dr ROBERT, was admitted as a Freeman of Belfast in 1725. [TBB]

SOFFRANE, Mr, in Belfast in 1645. [TBB]

THE PEOPLE OF BELFAST, 1600-1799

SOMERVILL, JAMES, a porter in Belfast, was admitted as a Freeman of Belfast in 1737. [TBB]

SORBY, JOHN, a laborer, was admitted as a Freeman of Belfast in 1658. [TBB]

SORBY, THOMAS, a laborer, was admitted as a Freeman of Belfast in 1658. [TBB]

SOUTH, JAMES, a gentleman in Belfast in 1659. [C]

SPANG, BESSIE, widow of Thomas Knox a merchant in Glasgow, formerly in Belfast, a deed, 1692. [NRS.RD3.77.465]

SPEARS, WILLIAM, master of the Salmon of Belfast 1689. [NRS.E72.19.15]; master of the Robert and John of Belfast in 1689. [NRS.E72.20.14]

SPEED, JOHN, was admitted as a Freeman of Belfast in 1641. [TBB]

SPENCE, ALEXANDER, son of John Spence of Blair, a merchant in Belfast, a deed, 1696. [NRS.RD3.86.263]

SPENCE, HUGH, a tailor, was admitted as a Freeman of Belfast in 1727. [TBB]

SPENCE, JOHN, of Blair, a merchant in Belfast, deeds, 1696. [NRS.RD3.86.150/263]

SPIER, SYMEON, was admitted as a Free Stapler of Belfast in 1637. [TBB]

SPOONER, ROBERT, a shoemaker, was admitted as a Freeman of Belfast in 1639. [TBB]

SPROULL, JOHN, in Belfast, 1669. [PRONI.T307A]

SPROULL, PATRICK, in Belfast, 1669. [PRONI.T307A]

SPROULL, ROBERT, in Belfast in 1645. [TBB]

THE PEOPLE OF BELFAST, 1600-1799

SPROULL, THOMAS, in Belfast, 1669. [PRONI.T307A]

SPRUSON, MICHAEL, a painter in Belfast, was admitted as a Freeman of Belfast in 1761. [TBB]

STAFFORD, RICHARD, sexton in Belfast in 1645. [TBB]

STAFFORD, WILLIAM, a mariner, was admitted as a Freeman of Belfast in 1728. [TBB]

STANTON, SAMUEL a burgess of Belfast, a letter 1754. [PRONI.D354.1007]

STARLING, PATRICK, was admitted as a Freeman of Belfast in 1640. [TBB]

STARNETT, JOHN, born 1762, died 1826, husband of Jane ...., born 1783, died 1827. [Shankill MI, Belfast]

STEELE, JAMES, in Belfast, 1669. [PRONI.T307A]

STEELE, JOHN, an adventurer who was granted land in the north-west-quarter of the barony of Belfast, 1643 [SPI.1642-1659: 354]

STEEL, MATTHEW, in Belfast, a lease in North Street, Belfast, in 1793. [PRONI.D298.85]

STEEL, ROBERT, master of the Neptune of Belfast in 1765. [NRS.E504.4.4]

STEENSON, ROBERT, in Belfast, 1669. [PRONI.T307A]; master of the Providence of Belfast 1669. [NRS.E72.12.1]

STEEL, ROBERT, in Belfast, lease in Union Street, Belfast, in 1796. [PRONI.D438.3]

STEPHENSON, JOHN, was admitted as a free burgess of Belfast, 1640. [TBB]

STEPHENSON, JOSEPH, a merchant in Belfast, witness to the will of Thomas McIlwain, 1777.

THE PEOPLE OF BELFAST, 1600-1799

STEVENSON, DAVID, a carman, was admitted as a Freeman of Belfast in 1727. [TBB]

STEVENSON, ELENOR, wife of John Brown a merchant in Belfast, died 1711. [Bangor Abbey MI]

STEVENSON, GEORGE, was admitted as a Freeman of Belfast in 1644. [TBB]

STEVENSON, JAMES, a co-partner of the Belfast Glass House Company, deed of partnership, 1791. [PRONI.]

STEVENSON, JOHN, in the Falls, was admitted as a Freeman of Belfast in 1730. [TBB]

STEVENSON, ROBERT, a burgess of Belfast in 1639. [TBB]

STEVENSON, THOMAS, was admitted as a Free Stapler of Belfast in 1640. [TBB]; Sovereign of Belfast 1642. [TBB]

STEVENSON, THOMAS, of the Falls of Belfast, was admitted as a Freeman of Belfast in 1737. [TBB]

STEVENSON, WILLIAM, a lease of Rosemary Lane, Belfast, 1787. [PRONI.CR3.32.B1.7]

STEWART, ALEXANDER, a merchant, was admitted as a Freeman of Belfast in 1729. [TBB]

STEWART, ANDREW, in Belfast, 1669. [PRONI.T307A]

STEWART, ANNE, born 1786, a spinster from Belfast, bound for Philadelphia aboard the <u>Commerce</u> in 1804. [BL.Addl.ms.]

STEWART, ARCHIBALD, in Belfast, 1669. [PRONI.T307A]

THE PEOPLE OF BELFAST, 1600-1799

STEWART, DAVID, a merchant in Belfast, aboard the gabart Ross of Belfast 1689-1690. [NRS.E72.3.20/21]

STEWART, EDWARD, a laborer, was admitted as a Freeman of Belfast in 1658, [TBB]; in Belfast, 1669. [PRONI.T307A]

STEWART, JAMES, a merchant, was admitted as a Free Commoner of Belfast in 1647. [TBB]; a merchant in Belfast in 1682. [PRONI.T420/97]

STEWART, JAMES, a councillor of Belfast, 1678. [TBB]

STEWART, JAMES, a merchant in Belfast, probate 1693. [PRONI.D1759/3B/1/71]

STEWART, JAMES, a merchant in Belfast, petitioned the Parliament of Scotland, 1689. [APS]; a deed, 1702. [NRS.RD3.99/2.34]

STEWART, JAMES, in Belfast, 1669; a deed, 1692. [PRONI.T307A; D509.32]

STEWART, JOHN, was admitted as a Freeman of Belfast in 1640. [TBB]; was admitted as a Free Stapler of Belfast in 1643, [TBB]; a merchant in Belfast, 1645. [TBB]

STEWART, JOHN, a merchant, was admitted as a Free Stapler and a Free Commoner of Belfast in 1647. [TBB]

STEWART, JOHN, in Belfast, 1669. [PRONI.T307A]

STEWART, JOHN, a councillor of Belfast, 1678. [TBB]

STEWART, JOHN, a merchant aboard the Alexander of Belfast 1683. [NRS.E72.12.7]

STEWART, JOHN, a merchant, was admitted as a Freeman of Belfast in 1727. [TBB]

THE PEOPLE OF BELFAST, 1600-1799

STEWART, RICHARD, vicar of Belfast Corporation Church in 1736.

STEWART, SAMUEL, a merchant in Belfast, was admitted as a Freeman of Belfast in 1760. [TBB]

STEWART, THOMAS, in Belfast, 1669. [PRONI.T307A]

STEWART, THOMAS, a yeoman in Belfast, witness to the will of John Buchanan, probate, 1784, Dublin.

STEWART, THOMAS, a lease of Rosemary Lane, Belfast, 1787. [PRONI.CR3.32.B1.7]

STEWART, WILLIAM, in Belfast, a deed, 1682. [NRS.RD4.50.183]

STEWART, WILLIAM, a wigmaker, was admitted as a Freeman of Belfast in 1746. [TBB]

STEWART, WILLIAM, a dealer in North Street, Belfast, was admitted as a Freeman of Belfast in 1748. [TBB]

STEWART, WILLIAM, a merchant in Belfast, was admitted as a Freeman of Belfast in 1758. [TBB]

STEWART, WILLIAM, in North Street, Belfast, a lease, 1770. [PRONI.D509.529]

STEWART, WILLIAM, born 1750, died 1811. [New Burying Ground MI]

STINSON, ROBERT, master and merchant of the Providence of Belfast 1669. [NRS.E72.12.1]

STINSON, Mrs, in Belfast in 1645. [TBB]

STIRLING, JAMES, of the Falls, a farmer, was admitted as a Freeman of Belfast in 1762, and was elected Sergeant at Mace in 1777. [TBB]

THE PEOPLE OF BELFAST, 1600-1799

STIRLING, WILLIAM, of the Falls, a farmer, was admitted as a Freeman of Belfast in 1762, and was elected Sergeant at Mace in 1777. [TBB]

STOKER, ANNA, a widow in Belfast, 1687. [NRS.CC8.8.78/512]

STOKER, THOMAS, in Belfast, a testament, 1688, Commissariat of Edinburgh. [NRS]

STORMONT, DAVID, born 1727, died 1814, husband of Mary....., born 1723, died 1783, parents of Thomas Stormont. [Shankill MI, Belfast]

STRACHAN, GEORGE, a yeoman and a rioter in Belfast, 1614. [OB.38]

STRAWBRIDGE, JOHN, master of the <u>Countess of Donegal of Belfast</u> trading with Charleston, South Carolina, in 1764. [TNA.CO5.511]

STOUT, ROBERT, master of the <u>Prince Charles of Belfast</u> trading with Jamaica in 1745. [NRS.E504.8.1]

STUCKLEY, WILLIAM, a gentleman in Belfast in 1659. [C]

STURDEY, JOHN, an adventurer who was granted land in the north-west-quarter of the barony of Belfast, 1643 [SPI.1642-1659: 354]

STYLES, SAMPSON, a Free Stapler of Belfast, 1635. [TBB]

SUFFERIN, ANDREW, a tailor, was admitted as a Freeman of Belfast in 1777. [TBB]

SUFFERIN, JAMES, a merchant, was admitted as a Freeman of Belfast in 1783. [TBB]

THE PEOPLE OF BELFAST, 1600-1799

SUMMERS, HENRY, master of the Mary of Belfast 1689. [NRS.E72.19.14]

SUTHERLAND, ALEXANDER, in Belfast, executor of Mary McWalters in Belfast, 1781. [PRONI.D199.10]

SUTHERLAND, GEORGE, in Belfast, 1750s. [PRONI.D354.872]

SYMKINS, HENRY, a chandler, was admitted as a Freeman of Belfast in 1638. [TBB]

TAFFE, Lieutenant Colonel THEOBALD, was admitted as a Free Stapler of Belfast in 1639. [TBB]

TATE, ALEXANDER, in Belfast, 1669. [PRONI.T307A]

TATE, HENRY, born 1772, died 1805. [Shankill MI, Belfast]

TATE.MATTHEW, a brazier, was admitted as a Free Commoner of Belfast in 1650. [TBB]

TAYLOR, ALEXANDER, a merchant, was admitted as a Free Commoner of Belfast in 1650. [TBB]

TAYLOR, JAMES, a flax dresser in Belfast, was admitted as a Freeman of Belfast in 1773. [TBB]

TAYLOR, JESSE, a merchant in Belfast, was admitted as a Freeman of Belfast in 1774. [TBB]

TAYLOR, JOHN, a shoemaker, was admitted as a Freeman of Belfast in 1730. [TBB]

TAYLOR, WILLIAM, in Belfast, a lease, 1770. [PRONI.D509.532]

TAYLOR, WILLIAM, a cabinetmaker, husband of Jane ....., born 1775, died 1811. [New Burying Ground MI]

THE PEOPLE OF BELFAST, 1600-1799

TEAT, THOMAS, of the Falls, was admitted as a Freeman of Belfast in 1771. [TBB]

TEAT, WILLIAM, a tailor, was admitted as a Freeman of Belfast in 1730. [TBB]

TEMPLETON, JOHN, born 1765, of Orange Grove, Malone, died 1825, husband of Katherine Johnstone, born 1773, died 1868. [New Burying Ground MI]

THEAKER, GEORGE, a burgess of Belfast in 1632. [TBB]

THEAKER, SAMPSON, in Belfast a grant of admonition, 1695. [PRONI.D298.1]; a gentleman burgess 1681-1692. [BMF]

THEAKER, THOMAS, a gentleman, was admitted as a burgess of Belfast in 1643. [TBB]; Sovereign of Belfast, 1648. [TBB]; [TCD.MS838,7-8]; died 1660, probate 1691.

THETFORD, ANTHONY, a merchant, was admitted as a Freeman of Belfast in 1725. [TBB]

THETFORD, FRANCIS, son of Francis Thetford, deceased, was admitted as a Free Commoner of Belfast in 1647, [PBB]; a merchant burgess 1665-1690. [BMF]

THETFORD, HENRY, a joiner, was admitted as a Free Commoner of Belfast in 1654, [TBB]; a burgess 1677-1678. [BMF]

THETFORD, VALENTINE, a cooper, was admitted as a Freeman of Belfast in 1730. [TBB]

THOM, WILLIAM, a merchant, was admitted as a Freeman of Belfast in 1639. [TBB]

THOMAS, ALEXANDER, clerk to Collyer and Company, was admitted as a Freeman of Belfast in 1730. [TBB]

THE PEOPLE OF BELFAST, 1600-1799

THOMSON, ALEXANDER, a burgess of Belfast in 1639. [TBB]

THOMSON, ALEXANDER, a cooper, was admitted as a Free Commoner of Belfast in 1652. [TBB]

THOMPSON, ALEXANDER, a maltster, was admitted as a Freeman of Belfast in 1746. [TBB]

THOMSON, GALLAN, a merchant in Belfast, 1770. [NRS.GD1.306]

THOMSON, GEORGE, an innkeeper in Belfast, was admitted as a Free Commoner of Belfast in 1645. [TBB]

THOMPSON, ISAAC, son of the Sovereign, was admitted as a Freeman of Belfast in 1772. [TBB]

THOMPSON, JAMES, a weaver in Belfast, a lease, 1731. [PRONI.D270.1]

THOMPSON, JAMES, a maltster in Belfast, was admitted as a Freeman of Belfast in 1774. [TBB]

THOMSON, JOHN, a shoemaker, was admitted as a Free Commoner of Belfast in 1650. [TBB]

THOMSON, JOHN, son of Alexander Thomson, was admitted as a Freeman of Belfast in 1641. [TBB]; in Belfast in 1645. [TBB]

THOMSON, JOHN, a merchant in Belfast, was admitted as a burgess and guilds-brother of Edinburgh in 1689 by right of his wife Bethia, daughter of James Inglis a merchant burgess and guilds-brother there. [EBR]

THOMPSON, JOSEPH, son of the Sovereign, was admitted as a Freeman of Belfast in 1772. [TBB]

THOMPSON, LEONARD, a merchant in Belfast, was admitted as a Free Stapler of Belfast in 1640. [TBB]

THE PEOPLE OF BELFAST, 1600-1799

THOMSON, LEWIS, a merchant in Belfast, 1628. [NRS.AC7.1.196]; Sovereign of Belfast in 1632. [TBB]

THOMSON, LEWIS, a saddler, son of Leonard Thomson deceased, was admitted as a Free Commoner of Belfast in 1655, [TBB]; a merchant burgess 1678-1708. [BMF]; petitioned the Privy Council of Scotland in 1691. [RPCS.XVI.309]

THOMSON, NICHOLAS, a gentleman, was admitted as a Free Stapler of Belfast in 1637. [TBB]

THOMPSON, RICHARD, son of the Sovereign, was admitted as a Freeman of Belfast in 1772. [TBB]

THOMSON, ROBERT, a burgess of Belfast in 1639. [TBB]

THOMPSON, ROBERT, a cooper, was admitted as a Freeman of Belfast in 1731. [TBB]

THOMSON, ROBERT, in Belfast, a letter, 1780. [PRONI.D562.]

THOMPSON, SHEM, in Belfast, a lease, 1770. [PRONI.D509.534]

THOMPSON, SHEM, jr., son of the Sovereign, was admitted as a Freeman of Belfast in 1772. [TBB]

THOMPSON, THOMAS, born 1766, died 1816, husband of Margaret, born 1761, died 1819. [New Burying Ground MI]

THOMSON, WILLIAM, was admitted as a burgess of Belfast, 1644. [TBB]

THOMPSON, WILLIAM, a merchant in Belfast, a lease, 1684. [PRONI.D654.R2.1]

THORNE, RICHARD, in Belfast, a deed, 1753. [PRONI.D695.44]

THE PEOPLE OF BELFAST, 1600-1799

THUNGER, EDWARD, was admitted as a Freeman of Belfast in 1640. [TBB]

TISDALL, HENRY, son of Reverend Dr William Tisdall, was admitted as a Freeman of Belfast in 1737. [TBB]

TINDALL, Reverend Dr WILLIAM, master of the Belfast Charity School, 1716. [PRONI.D509.39]; author of 'An account of the Charity School of Belfast' [Belfast, 1720]

TISDALL, Reverend WILLIAM, DD, vicar of Belfast Corporation Church in 1712.was admitted as a Freeman of Belfast in 1767. [TBB]

TISDALL, WILLIAM, in Belfast, a lease, 1770. [PRONI.D509.533]

TODD, ROSE, born 1707, died 1748, daughter of James Todd, and sister of James and Barbara. [Shankill MI, Belfast]

TODD, WILLIAM, a hardware merchant in Belfast, later in Wigtown, testament 1713, Commissariat of Wigtown. [NRS]

TOMLINSON, ROGER, was admitted as a Free Commoner of Belfast in 1647. [TBB]

TONRAGH, ROBERT, a shoemaker, was admitted as a Freeman of Belfast in 1725. [TBB]

TOOLEY, JOHN, an apothecary burgess, 1682-1687. [BMF]

TOOTELL, RICHARD, was admitted as a Freeman of Belfast in 1752. [TBB]

TOURAM, VICTOR, a peruke-maker, was admitted as a Freeman of Belfast in 1728. [TBB]

THE PEOPLE OF BELFAST, 1600-1799

TOWNSEND, WILLIAM, a tanner, was admitted as a Freeman of Belfast in 1727. [TBB]

TRAYLE, PATRICK, master of the Upton of Belfast trading with South Carolina in 1716-1717. [TNA.CO5.508]

TRELFORD, ISRAEL, born 1755, died 1811, husband of Jane ….[Shankill MI, Belfast]

TRIMBLE, N., master of the Fullwood of Belfast in 1661. [BMF]

UPTON, ARTHUR, in Castle Norton in the barony of Belfast in 1659. [C]

UPTON, HENRY, a burgess of Belfast in 1632. [TBB]

VAGHT, JOHN, a merchant in Belfast, was admitted as a Freeman of Belfast in 1761. [TBB]

VARNETT, HENRY, a tailor, was admitted as a Freeman of Belfast in 1726. [TBB]

VAUGHAN, JOHN, in County Donegal, was admitted as a Freeman of Belfast in 1730. [TBB]

VESEY, JOHN, was granted land on Broad Street, Belfast, 1616. [Inquisitionum in officio, ii.7]; a burgess of Belfast in 1632. [TBB]

VICAR, NEVIN, a ships carpenter, was admitted as a Freeman of Belfast in 1639. [TBB]; in Belfast in 1645. [TBB]

VICARY, RICHARD, a merchant, was admitted as a Freeman of Belfast in 1638. [TBB]

VILLARS, THOMAS, born 1763, died 1809, husband of Ruth …., born 1773, died 1818. [Shankill MI, Belfast]

THE PEOPLE OF BELFAST, 1600-1799

WALCOT, THOMAS, in Belfast, 1645. [TBB]; a gentleman burgess, 1660-1690. [BMF]

WALCOT, Mr, in Belfast in 1645. [TBB]

WALKER, JOHN, born 1667, a merchant from Belfast, emigrated via Liverpool to the Chesapeake in 1686. [LRO.QSP.625/2]

WALKER, JOSEPH, a shoemaker, was admitted as a Freeman of Belfast in 1639. [TBB]

WALKER, WILLIAM, in Belfast, grandson and heir of Andrew Walker a baillie of Dunfermline, Fife, 1717. [NRS.S/H]

WALKER, WILLIAM, a mariner, was admitted as a Freeman of Belfast in 1731. [TBB]

WALL, RICHARD, town clerk of Belfast, was admitted as a Freeman of Belfast in 1639. [TBB]

WALLACE, JAMES, born 1770, died 1826. [Shankill MI, Belfast]

WALLACE, MARTIN, born 1752, died 1817, husband of Margaret ...., born 1742, died 1803. [Shankill MI, Belfast]

WALLACE, ROBERT, born 1760, died 1841, husband of Margaret ....., born 1760, died 1823. [Shankill MI, Belfast]

WALL, RICHARD, town clerk of Belfast in 1646. [TBB]

WALLIS, Lieutenant Colonel JAMES, in the barony of Belfast, 1659. [C]

WALSH, CHARLES, a cooper, was admitted as a Freeman of Belfast in 1727. [TBB]

THE PEOPLE OF BELFAST, 1600-1799

WALSH, WILLIAM, was admitted as a Free Stapler of Belfast in 1635. [TBB]

WARD, MARCUS, died 1801, husband of Mary Shanks, died 1809. [New Burying Ground MI]

WARING, JOHN, was admitted as a Freeman of Belfast in 1644. [TBB]

WARING, THOMAS, a tanner, was admitted as a Free Stapler in Belfast in 1643; a burgess in 1652, [TBB]; Sovereign of Belfast from 1652-1655. [TBB]; a gentleman in Belfast, 1659. [C] a tanner/merchant burgess 1652-1665. [BMF]

WARING, WILLIAM, a tanner in Belfast, a gentleman in Belfast in 1659. [C]; a tanner and merchant burgess 1660-1677. [BMF]

WARK, JAMES, born 1658 in Scotland, a beef salter, died in Belfast in 1764. [FDJ.3833]

WARNOCK, GEORGE, in Belfast, a deed, 1796. [PRONI.D447.20]

WASHER, JOHN, a burgess of Belfast in 1639. [TBB]

WATERSON, THOMAS, a shoemaker, was admitted as a Freeman of Belfast in 1643. [TBB]

WATSON, JOHN, a merchant, was admitted as a Free Commoner of Belfast in 1650. [TBB]

WATSON, RINGAN, in Belfast in 1645. [TBB]

WATT, ROBERT or JAMES, a merchant, was admitted as a Freeman of Belfast in 1726. [TBB]

WATTS, SAMUEL, master of the <u>Alexander of Belfast</u> trading with Charleston, South Carolina, in1766. [TNA.CO5.511]

THE PEOPLE OF BELFAST, 1600-1799

WATT, WILLIAM, master of the Rose of Belfast 1690-1691. [NRS.E72.3.22; E72.12.18]

WEALLS, JOHN, a chapman, was admitted as a Freeman of Belfast in 1730. [TBB]

WEIR, JAMES, master of the Hanover of Belfast bound for Barbados in 1716, [WCI:9.2.1716]; bound for Italy, 1728. [PRONI.D354.474]

WEIR, JAMES, in Belfast, a lease of Millfield in Belfast, 1794. [PRONI.D298.87]

WEIR, ROBERT, a carman, was admitted as a Freeman of Belfast in 1727. [TBB]

WEIR, THOMAS, merchant on the Joan of Belfast bound for Barbados in 1716, and Madeira in 1691. [WCI.9.2.1716; 18.2.1716][NRS.E72.19.22]

WENMAN, PHILLIP, was admitted as a burgess of Belfast in 1640. [TBB]

WEST, JAMES, a tailor from Cumber, was admitted as a Freeman of Belfast in 1729. [TBB]

WESTFIELD, MATTHEW, a glazier, was admitted as a Freeman of Belfast in 1639. [TBB]

WHEATON, WILLIAM, was admitted as a Freeman of Belfast in 1641. [TBB]

WHEATS, JOHN, was admitted as a Sergeant of Belfast in 1655. [TSB]

WHEELAN, ABRAHAM, JOHN, a merchant in Belfast in 1754. [PRONI.D509.63]

WHINNERY, THOMAS, born 1760, postmaster of Belfast, died 1830. [New Burying Ground MI]

THE PEOPLE OF BELFAST, 1600-1799

WHITE, JOHN, a merchant in Belfast, aboard the Isobel of Belfast in 1667, [NRS.E72.9.3]

WHITE, JOHN, a carman, was admitted as a Freeman of Belfast in 1730. [TBB]

WHITE, ROBERT, master of the Alexander of Belfast 1683-1685, also of the Anna Helena of Belfast in 1689. [NRS.E72.12.7/10/15]

WHITEHEAD, JOHN, of Belfast, aboard the Content of Belfast trading with France in 1681. [SPDom.1681.228]; a slave in Turkey 1692. [GSU.11]

WHITESAL, THOMAS, a burgess of Belfast, a letter 1754. [PRONI.D354.1007]

WHITESIDE, DUKE, of the Falls, was admitted as a Freeman of Belfast in 1771. [TBB]

WHITESIDE, ROBERT, a felt-maker, was admitted as a Freeman of Belfast in 1639. [TBB]

WHITESIDE, R., master of the Charlmont of Belfast in 1681-1685. [BMF]

WHITLOCK, CHARLES, was admitted as a Free Commoner of Belfast in 1651. [TBB]

WHITLOCK, JAMES, a peruke-maker, was admitted as a Freeman of Belfast in 1726. [TBB]

WHITLOCK, MICHAEL, a peruke-maker, was admitted as a Freeman of Belfast in 1728. [TBB]

WHITTLE, JAMES, born 1780, died 1820. [New Burying Ground MI]

WILKISON, JOHN, a burgess of Belfast in 1639. [TBB]

THE PEOPLE OF BELFAST, 1600-1799

WILLIAMS, LYDIA, born 1750, died 1822. [Shankill MI, Belfast]

WILLIAMSON, EDWARD, master of the Roebuck of Belfast 1690. [NRS.E72.19.18]

WILLIAMSON, GEORGE, a butcher, was admitted s a Free Commoner of Belfast in 1650. [TBB]

WILLIAMSON, GEORGE, master of the Salmon of Belfast 1688. [NRS.E72.19.15]

WILLIAMSON, JAMES, born 1756, residing in James Place, Belfast, died 1832, husband of Barbara ……, born 1766, died 1840. [New Burying Ground MI]

WILLIAMSON, JAMES, of the Falls, was admitted as a Freeman of Belfast in 1771. [TBB]

WILLIAMSON, JOHN, master of the Isaac of Belfast trading with Charleston, South Carolina, in 1733-1734. [TNA.CO5.509][SCGaz:23.2.1734]

WILLIAMSON, NEVIN, of the Falls, was admitted as a Freeman of Belfast in 1771. [TBB]

WILLIAMSON, THOMAS, born 1624, died 1712. [Shankill MI, Belfast]

WILLOUGHBY, JOHN, a gentleman in Belfast, died 1640. [TBB]

WILLOX, JOHN, in Belfast, 1669. [PRONI.T307A]

WILLS, ROBERT, a postmaster in Belfast, 1754. [PRONI.D270.5]; a burgess of Belfast, a letter 1754. [PRONI.D354.1007]

WILLS, ROBERT, jr.a hardware merchant in Belfast, a burgess of Belfast, a letter 1754. [PRONI.D354.1007];

THE PEOPLE OF BELFAST, 1600-1799

later trading with Pennsylvania in 1760s.
[Familia.19.64-73]

WILSON, CHARLES, a gardener, was admitted as a Freeman of Belfast in 1729. [TBB]

WILSON, EDWARD, a burgess of Belfast, a letter 1754. [PRONI.D354.1007]

WILSON, HENRY, born 1779, a schoolmaster from Belfast, bound for Philadelphia aboard the snow George of Philadelphia in 1803. [BL.Addl.ms]

WILSON, HILL, Customs Collector of Belfast, was admitted as a burgess of Belfast in 1752, [TBB]; a letter 1754. [PRONI.D354.1007]

WILSON, HUGH, a merchant in Belfast, was admitted as a burgess and guilds-brother of Ayr in 1722, [ABR]

WILSON, HUGH, born 1747, a merchant in Belfast, died 1822. [New Burying Ground MI]

WILSON, JAMES, in Belfast, a bond, 1790. [PRONI.D491.50]

WILSON, JOHN, master of the Providence of Belfast 1686. [NRS.E72.12.13]

WILSON, JOHN, a yeoman in Belfast, witness to the will of James Smith, probate 1720, Dublin.

WILSON, JOHN, a merchant, was admitted as a Freeman of Belfast in 1731. [TBB]

WILSON, JOHN, a blacksmith, was admitted as a Freeman of Belfast in 1731. [TBB]

WILSON, JOHN, a merchant in Belfast, was admitted as a burgess and guilds-brother of Ayr in 1738. [ABR]

THE PEOPLE OF BELFAST, 1600-1799

WILSON, JOSEPH, born 1781, a dealer from Belfast, bound for Philadelphia aboard the snow George of Philadelphia in 1803. [BL.Addl.ms]

WILSON, LANCELOT, a merchant in Belfast, was admitted as a burgess and guilds-brother of Glasgow, 1719. [GBR]; also as a burgess and guilds-brother of Ayr in 1719. [ABR]

WILSON, NATHANIEL, a merchant in Belfast, a lease, 1726, [PRONI.D270.1]; in Belfast 1727. [NRS.GD10.466]

WILSON, NATHANIEL, grandson of the Sovereign Stephen Haven, a merchant in Belfast, was admitted as a Freeman of Belfast in 1760. [TBB]

WILSON, RALPH, was admitted as a Freeman of Belfast in 1796. [TBB]

WILSON, ROBERT, master of the John of Belfast 1689. [NRS.E72.3.19]

WILSON, ROBERT, a merchant in Belfast, was admitted as a burgess and guilds-brother of Glasgow in 1703. [GBR]; a merchant in Belfast, trading with Cadiz, Spain, 1712. [PRONI.D354.359]; trading with America, 1717, [PRONI.D354.363]; was admitted as a burgess and guilds-brother of Ayr in 1713, [ABR]; a lease of the Old Gate House in Belfast, 1717, [PRONI.D509.43];1722, [NRS.AC9.849]

WILSON, ROBERT, master of the Prince of Wales of Belfast , 1760s. [SCGaz.1539/1540/1654]

WILSON, STEPHEN, grandson of the Sovereign Stephen Haven, a merchant in Belfast, was admitted as a Freeman of Belfast in 1760. [TBB]

THE PEOPLE OF BELFAST, 1600-1799

WILSON, THOMAS, an apprentice to Archibald McNeile an apothecary in Belfast, 1720, witness to the will of Richard Hodgkinson probate Dublin, 1720.

WILSON, WILLIAM, the younger, a butcher in Belfast, 1622. [TBB]

WILSON, WILLIAM, master of the <u>Donegal of Belfast</u> trading with Catelonia, 1705. [SPDom.42.119.193]

WILSON, WILLIAM, a merchant in Belfast, was admitted as a burgess and guilds-brother of Ayr in 1713. [ABR]

WILSON, WILLIAM, a merchant in Belfast, was admitted as a Freeman of Belfast in 1760. [TBB]

WIRES, JAMES, master of the <u>Hanover of Belfast</u> 1717. [TNA.CO5.508]

WIRLING, ANN, born 1730, died 1810. [New Burying Ground Belfast]

WIRLING, ROBERT, born 1758, died 1823. [New Burying Ground MI]

WISDOM, HENRY, a currier, was admitted as a Free Commoner of Belfast in 1647. [TBB]

WISELY, ARCHIBALD, in Bangor, was admitted as a Freeman of Belfast in 1737. [TBB]

WOODS, EDWARD, was admitted as a Freeman of Belfast in 1641. [TBB]

WOODS, MICHAEL, senior, a yeoman at the Falls, Belfast, a bond 1678. [NRS.GD10.823]

WOOD, RICHARD, an adventurer who was granted land in the south-west-quarter of the barony of Belfast, 1643. [SPI.1642-1659: 354]

THE PEOPLE OF BELFAST, 1600-1799

WOODBURN, WILLIAM, a cooper, was admitted as a Freeman of Belfast in 1776. [TBB]; born 1730, died 1808. [New Burying Ground MI]

WOODRUFFE, JAMES, a gentleman, was admitted as a Free Stapler of Belfast in 1637. [TBB]

WOODS, DAVID, born 1767, a merchant in Belfast, died 1807. [New Burying Ground MI]

WOODS, ECCLES, of the Falls, was admitted as a Freeman of Belfast in 1747. [TBB]

WOODS, HILL, of the Falls, was admitted as a Freeman of Belfast in 1771. [TBB]

WOODS, JAMES, of the Falls, was admitted as a Freeman of Belfast in 1771. [TBB]

WOODS, JOHN, of the Falls, was admitted as a Freeman of Belfast in 1771. [TBB]

WOODS, MARY, born 1756, died 1802. [New Burying Ground MI]

WOODS, MICHAEL, of the Falls, was admitted as a Freeman of Belfast in 1771. [TBB]

WOODS, WHITESIDE, of the Falls, was admitted as a Freeman of Belfast in 1771. [TBB]

WORKMAN, JOHN, born 1776, died 1846, husband of Helen ....., born 1780, died 1859. [New Burying Ground MI, Belfast]

WORTHINGTON, BRUEN, a butcher, was admitted as a Freeman of Belfast in 1728. [TBB]

WORTHINGTON, MARTIN, a butcher, was admitted as a Freeman of Belfast in 1728. [TBB]

THE PEOPLE OF BELFAST, 1600-1799

WORTHINGTON, WILLIAM, a butcher, was admitted as a Freeman of Belfast in 1728. [TBB]

WRAY, Sir WILLIAM, was admitted as a Free Stapler of Belfast in 1640. [TBB]

WRIGHT, Mrs MARIAN, spouse of John Wright, banished from Belfast in 1640 for keeping a disorderly house. [TBB]

WYE, GILBERT, a gentleman in Belfast, 1659, [C]; of the Church of Ireland, a burgess of Belfast from 1662 to 1680. [BMF]

WYLLIE, JOHN, a merchant in Belfast, was admitted as a burgess and guilds-brother of Ayr in 1718. [ABR]

YOUNG, ALEXANDER, a merchant in Belfast, a lease, 1726. [PRONI.D270.1]

YOUNG, CHARLES, a merchant, was admitted as a burgess of Belfast in 1730, [TBB]; a letter 1754. [PRONI.D354.1007]

YOUNG, ELIZABETH, a widow in Belfast, a lease in 1754, and in 1783. [PRONI.D509.64; D270.11]

YOUNG, HUGH, a merchant in Belfast, a lease, 1726. [PRONI.D270.1]; a merchant, was admitted as a Freeman of Belfast in 1728. [TBB]

YOUNG, JAMES, was admitted as a Freeman of Belfast in 1727. [TBB]

YOUNG, JAMES, a merchant, was admitted as a Freeman of Belfast in 1731. [TBB]

YOUNG, JOHN, in Belfast, 1685. [NRS.GD10.832]

YOUNG, JOHN, a merchant in Belfast, probate 1724, Dublin

THE PEOPLE OF BELFAST, 1600-1799

YOUNG, LENNOX, son of Alexander Young a merchant in Belfast, matriculated at Glasgow University in 1744. [MAGU.3]

YOUNG, Miss MARTHA, in Belfast, a deed, 1800. [PRONI.D270.20]

YOUNG, MARTHA, born 1713, wife of Thomas Coulter, died 1740, their son John Young, born 1731, died 1739. [Shankill MI, Belfast]

YOUNG, NATHANIEL, in Belfast, 1727. [NRS.GD10.488]

YOUNG, ROBERT, in Belfast, 1685. [NRS.GD10.832]

YOUNG, SAMUEL, merchant on the Janet of Belfast 1691. [NRS.E72.19.21]

SOURCES

ABR	=	Ayr Burgess Roll
ACA	=	Aberdeen City Archives
ActsPCCol		Acts of the Privy Council, Colonial
AD	=	Alumni Dublinsis
APS	=	Acts of the Parliaments of Scotland
BL	=	British Library
BMF	=	Belfast Merchant Families
BNL	=	Belfast Newsletter
C	=	Census

THE PEOPLE OF BELFAST, 1600-1799

CDG	=	Charters and documents relating to Glasgow
CTB	=	Calendar of Treasury Books
EBR	=	Edinburgh Burgess Roll
EUL	=	Edinburgh University Library
EWJ	=	Edinburgh Weekly Journal
FDJ	=	Faulkner's Dublin Journal
GBR	=	Glasgow Burgess Roll
GM	=	Gentleman's Magazine
GSU	=	General Synod of Ulster
HSPa	=	Historical Society of Pennsylvania
IWD	=	Index of Will Extracts, Dublin
LRO	=	Liverpool Record Office
MAGU	=	Matriculation Albums of Glasgow University
MI	=	Monumental Inscription
NAI	=	National Archives of Ireland
NARA	=	National Archives Records Administration
NLS	=	National Library of Scotland
NNQ	=	Northern Notes and Queries
NRS	=	National Records of Scotland
OB	=	Old Belfast
P	=	Prisoners of the '45
PaGaz	=	Pennsylvania Gazette
PCC	=	Prerogative Court of Canterbury

THE PEOPLE OF BELFAST, 1600-1799

RPCS	=	Register of the Privy Council of Scotland
REA	=	Register of Edinburgh Apprentices
SCGaz	=	South Carolina Gazette
SM	=	Scots Magazine
SPAWI	=	Calendar State Papers, America and the West Indies
SPDom		Calendar of State Papers, Domestic
SPI	=	Calendar of State Papers, Ireland
StABR	=	St Andrews Burgess Roll
TBB	=	The Town Book of the Corporation of Belfast, 1613-1816, r m young, Belfast 1892
TNA	=	The National Archives, London
UJA	=	Ulster Journal of Archaeology
VaGaz	=	Virginia Gazette
WCI	=	West Country Intelligence

www.ingramcontent.com/pod-product-compliance
Lightning Source LLC
Chambersburg PA
CBHW072141160426
43197CB00012B/2193